Hunting Blunders
and
The One That Got Away!

Gerry Caillouet

Forward By Steve Chapman

With Contributions Written By:
Charlie Alsheimer, Bill D. Blackman, Steve Chapman, Jim Grassi, Larry D. Jones, Larry W. Jones, T. R. Michaels, Dr. Tom Rakow, Ken Reed, Dwight Schuh, Gerald Shaffner, Bill Snodgrass, Russell Thornberry and Dave Watson.

Miami Graphics Services, Inc.
West Milton, Ohio 45383

Hunting Blunders
and
The One That Got Away!

International Standard Book Number 0-9679032-1-1
Library of Congress Card Number 00-103420
All Rights Reserved
Manufactured in the United States of America

Miami Graphic Services, Inc.
West Milton, Ohio

DEDICATION

To my wife Cyndi,
Without her faithfulness, love, and hard work this book, the radio program, and daily operation of God's Great Outdoors would not be possible. You complete me.

And
To the arrows in my quiver, our two wonderful sons, Courtney and Clinton and my favorite daughter Katie. I pray your walk with God leaves me in a trail of dust.

And
The God who makes Cyndi and I one. He opens doors we have never dreamed existed. Praise be to our Lord and Savior Jesus Christ!

Listen to God's Great Outdoors weekly program anytime, anywhere on the web page: www.ggoutdoors.org

God's Great Outdoors

8193 Emerick Road
West Milton, OH 45383
(937) 698-3656

Cover Photo By:	upper photo - Gerry Caillouet
	lower photo - © Charles J. Alsheimer
Cover Design By:	Tim Parmenter and Gerry Caillouet

Back Cover Photo By:	upper photo - Tim Parmenter
	lower photo - Jerry Robinson
Back Cover Background By:	*REALTREE* ® X-TRA™ GREY
Back Cover Design By:	Tim Parmenter and Gerry Caillouet

ACKNOWLEDGMENTS

First, I want to thank my wife, Cyndi for her typing, ideas, and the work of compiling this material. This has been a project years in the making. Next, I want to let my daughter, Katie, know how much I appreciate her editing of the essays and cleaning up for reading sake, the radio scripts used in this book. Then I want to acknowledge and thank Pastor Jack Peters who added ideas and checked scriptural correctness and content. Thanks to Tim Parmenter at Miami Graphics, who picked up this book project and ran with it as if it were his own, and of course thanks to everyone else who works at my hometown printer. A thank you to both Jerry Robinson and Charles J. Alsheimer for their photography work. Also, thanks to my two friends at Realtree, Larry Bridgeman and Keith Jennings for permission to use the Realtree Camouflage Pattern on the book's back cover. Also, a special thank you to all those who gave financially to the book project. Only time will reveal how many lives have been impacted. And of course many thanks to all the sportsmen who were willing to let the rest of the world peek into their less than perfect lives. Last, thanks to my Board of Directors for your dedication, wisdom, and encouragement. This is as much your book as it is mine.

Board of Directors: Pastor Steve Peters
Douglas Henness
Steve Chapman
Ken Beck
Denver Crowell
Larry W. Jones

TABLE OF CONTENTS

FORWARD

I'll never forget the afternoon I arrived at the edge of a lush, winter wheat field with my portable treestand. I was especially excited about the hunt because it was my very first time to go after the illusive whitetail using a pistol. The field held great potential for a sighting and I was definitely keyed up. The tree I found to ascend was not ideal because it had quite a few small branches that had to be cut away as I maneuvered my way up. I got quite involved in the process but after about fifteen minutes of vigorous trimming I was finally ready to settle in and enjoy the vigil.

About 4:15 a really nice buck appeared on the opposite side of the field. With about forty-five minutes of shooting light remaining, I nervously watched him as he slowly fed my way. My heart was pounding as he gradually turned and headed toward the opening I hoped he would use in order to enter the acorn laden woods behind me. Unfortunately, he had consumed enough time that the proverbial window for my shot opportunity was quickly closing.

As if the deer knew I was in the tree, he waited until the lights went out before he finally came in close enough for pistol range. He was just a dark form in the field and I knew a shot was neither wise nor legal. I let him pass and listened as he wandered off into the distance. Then I reluctantly began my dismount.

After detaching my stand and gathering my gear, I stood at the bottom of the tree and thought to myself, "I should unload my gun for safety's sake before I go traipsing off into the woods." That's when I discovered something that left me shaking my head in a mixture of disgust and laughter. I opened the cylinder of my pistol and found it was empty! Duh! In all my tree trimming and settling in processes, I had overlooked the main ingredient when it comes to sending a bullet toward a "wall hanger." I failed to load my gun! I could almost hear the loud metal to metal snap, minus the bang, if I had pulled the hammer back and attempted a shot. What a "bummer" that would have been.

When I finished sufficiently kicking myself for being so absentminded, I began to laugh. I admit I debated whether or not to tamper with my reputation by telling my buddies about my stupidity. But...I've never been known to hold back any tale that might spoon out a little of one of life's best medicines. Laughter does good to a soul.

When I did tell my friends they didn't laugh at me...they laughed *with* me. In fact, they were so inspired and refreshed by the opportunity to chuckle about my "live and learn" moment that they were willing to divulge some of their own foul-ups. It was some of the best fellowship we ever had.

Perhaps, you could use some of that kind of fellowship, a time with others who love the outdoors. If so, then the book you hold in your hands is a timely offering to your soul. These pages are filled with the kind of stories you just read. My friend Gerry Caillouet has made the careful effort to not only compile a whole bushel of tales from "red-faced" hunters, like me, but he has also added some valuable insights that life's failures can yield.

I suggest you read these delightful and short chapters to your family. It will be time well spent. And, take this book to a hunting or fishing camp, or on any excursion. It will add joy to the journey as you share in the lives of those who have been open enough to admit imperfection. Now, turn to the page and let the healing begin!

Steve Chapman

The Trail Head

*Three Things You Need To Know Before You Start Down
This Trail To Adventure*

First, for your information, the idea for the hunting blunders used on the weekly twenty-five minute nationally syndicated radio broadcast I host and produce came from reading Dwight Schuh's book *Hunting Open-Country Mule Deer.* The editor of BOWHUNTER Magazine is incredibly frank in this book he has authored on pursuing mule deer, about hunting mistakes he has made. I could see how sharing in this way was meant to teach, but I saw that it could also help other hunters realize we are all on a level plain. What I mean is, just because Dwight and others make their living in the outdoors doesn't shield them from being human. We all can blow it. What amazed me was how many of the true stories about foul-ups I've been told, have been something I've done or wish I hadn't done. I believe the same thing may happen to you. Also, as I began writing and airing the hunting blunders, the fishing mistakes just naturally followed. After all, there are over twice as many fishermen as hunters, leaving more room for error.

Second, the *Hunting Blunders and One That Got Away!* stories were not written to be read in a book, but voiced for radio production on God's Great Outdoors. It may be as you read the copies of script you'll discover what would constitute a grammatical error. However, what you read and what is aired on the radio are not one and the same. When Jon Skillman, one of the most gifted voices in radio today reads these for production, he has the freedom to add pauses or voice inflection changes wherever he feels the story will be benefitted dramatically or for the humor of the moment. I didn't want to subject the already voiced blunders to changes just for the sake of compiling them into a book. So, if you find a run-on sentence or punctuation error, and the use of improper grammar is your pet peeve, please accept my apology. Try if you will to understand what "The Hunting Blunders" and "One That Got Away" stories are, radio broadcast manuscript. Plus, they are written by a guy who five years ago knew nothing about radio or writing such things. That's part of the miracle of my being on the radio as you'll discover at this book's end. (Also, if you're an English teacher this is my revenge for putting me through the tortures of diagraming sentences - just kidding - sort of.)

Last and most important, there are thirty-one personal thoughts I've written, one accompanying each pair of blunders. This will allow you if you choose, to use the book for one month as a devotional. *But if you are not so inclined to read these spiritually directed essays and just want to experience the fishing foul-ups and hunting boo-boo's, by all means feel free to skip them, you have my permission.* I hope you'll truly enjoy reading *Hunting Blunders and The One That Got Away!*

Gerry Caillouet

Day One
HERE'S A: "ONE THAT GOT AWAY"
FISHING STORY FROM
"God's Great Outdoors"
#016

Here's a story that really stinks, literally! Russell Thornbery, the Executive Editor of *Buckmaster* magazine, hasn't always made his living as an outdoor writer and editor. Besides a short time as a professional musician, Russ spent many years outfitting and guiding fishermen and hunters in Canada.

One summer Russell was guiding two fly fishermen for trout, on the famous Bow River. This water course flows out of the Canadian Rockies and on to the prairies of southern Alberta. Things were not going well at all. Russell said, "You could not even buy a fish, it was that bad! High winds plowing across the prairie making it very tough to cast a fly rod. It would have been tough for an expert, which neither of the men were. Stopping for lunch, the discouraged fishermen lay down to take a nap after eating."

Now normally, Russell didn't fish while guiding his clients, but he waded out while the guys rested. He hoped if he could catch a fish, it would renew their spirits and belief that trout really did exist in the Bow River.

Going down to a section of the river where the grass bank formed a high wall on one side of the water way, Russ gave it his best. However, the wind was overpowering his efforts and whipping his back casts onto the grassy bank. He'd been hung up a half dozen times or so when he felt the line snag the bank of prairie grass behind him again. Responding with a very hard jerk to free the line, the line gave, yet it felt as if something ...... well something felt funny. Russell turned to see a ball of black and white fur flying down off the bank and heading right on top of him. He ducked in time as a poor old skunk he now had on his line sailed by and landed in the river! Russ now thinks the skunk mistook the big streamer fly for a grasshopper and as he tried to grab it, it grabbed him only to become his demise.

Now Russell Thornberry may have been skunked on that fishing expedition, but one place he wasn't, and that's where it came to his eternal future after his death. You too can have assurance of peace for the life hereafter. For a booklet on the subject by Hank Parker titled "More Than Winning and Losing" and Jim Grassi's "The Ultimate Fishing Challenge," contact us here by mail, phone, or e-mail at God's Great Outdoors, they are both, free to you!

HERE'S A:
"MY BIGGEST HUNTING BLUNDER" FROM
"God's Great Outdoors"
#001

As the host of a Christian radio program known as, God's Great Outdoors, Gerry Caillouet remembers a time emotions overran clear thinking and cost him a whitetail buck. Some years back he was shotgun hunting an old logging road that cut along the side of a ridge in the hills of southeast Ohio.

"I was still hunting up a logging road, the prevailing wind was in my face and deer sign was everywhere. It was a perfect day to still hunt, wet leaves and an overcast sky, with occasional spitting of snow showers. At midday I was halfway up the road when a nice 8 point buck descended off the ridge top. He headed toward the breeding scrape located where the old road and ridge met. When the buck stopped just before dropping onto the flat, I prepared to shoot. But a sapling blocked a clear shot. The buck stepped down out of view and forced me to move up the old road to a rise where I could clearly see the buck in easy shotgun range. Why I didn't shoot then I still can't say, but I believe I just forgot I had a shotgun and felt the need to close the yardage, as if in bowhunting.

"Moving to close the gap, the next section of road dipped down, removing all visual contact. As I came up out of the road's depression, suddenly I was in full view of the rutting buck. I was focused too much on the trail and keeping quiet. I saw the buck at the same time the deers' head was coming up and his lips were curled back, sniffing my scent. The air was swirling and the buck winded me, then spotted me too! Emotion rushed upon me and screamed 'Shoot! He's about to break and you'll lose him!'

"The buck spun around and headed across the overgrown logging road. Leading the deer too far, I fired two quick shots in front of the buck. Then my brain began yelling at my runaway emotions, 'What are you doing? At this distance you should aim dead on!' So, swinging the gun sight onto the buck's chest, I followed the deer as he ran. Squeezing off a shot, Boom! A ten inch diameter poplar took a direct hit as the buck ran between the tree and myself. The eight pointer then disappeared as it dropped off the logging road and escaped by descending down the tree choked ridge. I kicked myself many times for blowing that hunt, but now I can laugh at it...almost."

Gerry may have missed the mark on that hunt, but one hunting trip he didn't miss out on was the hunt for eternal life through Jesus Christ. You also can find success in the ultimate of hunts, the one for eternal salvation.

For a free booklet by Charlie Alsheimer called, "The Ultimate Hunt," contact us here at God's Great Outdoors by mail, phone, or e-mail and we will be sure to see that you receive one. You will also receive a free copy of "The Greatest Hunt of All," by Dwight Schuh.

"Show Me The Money!"
#001

One of the comments I've heard time and again is, "The Bible is just another book. Perhaps it was once important, but not today. Maybe even God inspired, but only given as a benchmark, a guide if you will, to help us govern and live our lives." In other words, a place to start from, but nothing set in stone. As times have changed, so has how we should view the Bible.

I know, because before Christ changed my life, I remember saying such things. Yet, I can say now after reading through God's inspired and infallible word a number of times, such statements are all... well, they smell like a wet skunk. Fact is, if someone believes the bible to be a book of lies, half-truths or just outdated directions for some other time, why not prove those claims? It is my understanding, that a number of book publishing companies have a standing offer to pay ten million dollars to anyone who brings them just the rough draft of a book disproving the Bible. With the Holy Bible being the top selling book year after year, a book exposing the Bible as a fraud, would sell as they say, "like hotcakes!" The author of such a book would be rich, as the royalties would come rolling in, and don't forget the television appearances! The thing is, when someone tries to do this, their plan takes on the form of the number two selling book of all times, as it's *Gone With The Wind*.

1 Corinthians 1:18
"For the message of the cross is foolishness to those who are perishing, but to us who are being saved it is the power of God."

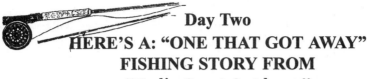

Day Two
HERE'S A: "ONE THAT GOT AWAY"
FISHING STORY FROM
"God's Great Outdoors"
#002

Al Lindner and brother, Ron, co-founders of *In-Fisherman*, have created the largest information network for supplying fishing knowledge. They cover walleye to catfish, dispensing information to fishermen worldwide. The *In-Fisherman* magazine, the *In- Fisherman* TV and radio show, books, videos and other products entertain and educate all who enjoy wetting a line.

Several years ago, Al was shooting a commercial for a well-known fishing line manufacturer. The TV spot would have Al leaning over a branch and pulling this big bass out of heavy cover saying, "I can't believe a line this thin can be this strong!"

Al begins, "It was a late autumn shoot and they had brought in the full New York TV crew, very high-dollar stuff, to shoot a 30-second commercial. The bass boat was next to a dead tree they had selected for the scene. I leaned out of the boat, over the branch in ready to pull the fish out of the heavy cover with the line in hand."

The director gave the crew word to begin filming. And as he barked out the all familiar "action" something unexpected happened. As the cameras rolled, the limb that Al was leaning on over the water broke, sending him plunging into the frigid water. As Al emerged soaking wet, he had his bass in hand. With lights blazing down on him he realized the cameras were still rolling. Being the true professional that he is, he delivered his lines and then started laughing.

At this point, the director asked the cameraman, "Did you get that?" To which he replied, "Yes!" So the director, satisfied with the footage yelled, "That's a take! Let's go home!" and they packed up and headed back to New York.

That commercial was one of the funniest misadventures you will ever see and it all just happened. This commercial was used for many years - it was that good. Anyone watching it was unaware that it was totally unrehearsed. It did go on and win a national award.

Now Al Lindner may have laughed at the situation he found himself in that day, but one thing Al does not take as a joke is his position with God and knowing he has eternal life in Jesus Christ. You can be sure of your position too! For a free booklet on the subject by Hank Parker titled, "More Than Winning and Losing," call, write or e-mail us here at God's Great Outdoors. We will also send you a copy of "The Ultimate Fishing Challenge," by Jim Grassi.

HERE'S A:
"MY BIGGEST HUNTING BLUNDER" FROM
"God's Great Outdoors"
#002

Burley Hall is a 3-D archery world and national champion who is also employed by *High Country Bows*. His hunting blunder was what you call a series of mistakes, some of which he'd relive over and over. Not just because they'd stuck in the recesses of his mind, but because the video camcorder was running to capture what was supposed to be a successful hunt.

It happened on one of those plain, nice, sunny, frosty mornings. Burley and the camera crew were filming the action as it unfolded. Now Burley had already missed another deer earlier in the week, something most everyone cannot imagine could happen to a professional 3-D archer. At least one who has won a number of national titles. But here he was again with his bow at full draw on a very large doe, hoping to put some venison in the freezer and contribute footage to the production being filmed. At this close range he shouldn't miss, but he second guessed himself. Burley was about to squeeze the trigger on his bow string release when he said to himself, "Bring another pin down." So, he lowered his bow sight to the next pin and released. The late October frost-covered leaves under the doe danced as the arrow sailed into direct contact with a very large object, the planet earth! But God would allow Burley success as the doe only ran a short distance and made the fatal mistake of giving the opportunity for a second shot. This time Burley Hall's arrow was dead-on.

Now Burley Hall may have been given a second chance to harvest a whitetail doe that clear October morning, but you can't count on a second chance to receive Jesus Christ as Lord and Savior. God's Word tells us "Today is the day of salvation." No one can be sure of tomorrow, for our days are like the smoke from a camp fire, here a moment then gone. So why not have the peace that passes all understanding? The peace that only eternal life in Jesus Christ can bring. Burley Hall has that peace, and you can too! For a free booklet on the subject by Charlie Alsheimer, called "The Ultimate Hunt," just write, call, or E-mail us here at God's Great Outdoors and we'll be glad to send you a copy. You'll also be sent a free copy of "The Greatest Hunt of All," by Dwight Schuh.

"It's No Titanic!"
#002

Now, would you like to fish or hunt everyday, anywhere in the world that your little heart desires? How wealthy could an author become with a book showing the Bible to be a hoax? Well, one recent count showed 60 million Bibles and 90 million New Testaments printed each year. A member of "The Gideon Society" shared with me that they distribute a million copies a week around the world. Let's say that the publisher of your book which disproves the Bible, besides the ten million dollars, gives you only fifty cents a copy for each book sold. And, your book only sells one-fourth of as many copies the first year as the Bible. Plus, if you've done your research, the proof you present stands up and sales increase annually. Just think of it - all your dreams come true! So, what are you waiting for? Go ahead and try to disprove it if you believe the Bible is a lie.

Others have attempted to, but not just for money. The highly educated and brilliant Cambridge University professor, C.S. Lewis' skepticism ended as he examined the evidence about Jesus Christ and the Bible. And there's Josh McDowell, a rebellious college student who was told by one of his teachers he was "straight 'D' student material." This angered Josh to the point of causing him to redirect his life with a plan of serious study to disprove the faculty member. His life's goal included law school and local political service ending with the position of Michigan's governor within twenty-five years. But on the path of his redirected life, this now student leader and skeptic of God's existence, was challenged to intellectually examine the claims of Christians about Jesus Christ. Adding this to his list of goals, he set out to reveal the lie. However, his serious studies resulted in the opposite, and he became a Christian himself. His book, *Evidence That Demands A Verdict* (Here's Life Publishers Inc.) is the result of his research and is loaded with facts, cover-to-cover. So, while trying to sink others' faith, he climbed aboard what the world considers "A ship of fools!"

Hebrews 4:12
"For the word of God is living and active. Sharper than any double-edged sword, it penetrates even to dividing soul and spirit, joints and marrow; it judges the thoughts and attitudes of the heart."

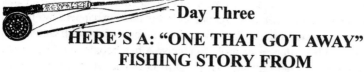

Day Three
HERE'S A: "ONE THAT GOT AWAY"
FISHING STORY FROM
"God's Great Outdoors"
#003

With the beauty of God's creation all around him as he grew to be a man, it's no wonder Michael Card enjoys the outdoors so much. Michael lived in the middle of Tennessee, but spent much time in the scenic high country of the eastern part of his home state. He became a serious hiker at age 14 and pursued it at every chance on through college. His treks took him to the Blue Ridge and Smokey Mountains and on the Appalachian Trail. College life was a blast as Michael was a member of the school's shooting team and his studies soared in the direction of forestry, with a goal of one day doing bird counts for the U.S. Forestry Service. But, amidst all the outdoor interests was still his love of music and it was this passion that eventually became the path he would travel on through life. His goal in writing his music is to teach God's word. It has been this singer and song writer's journey now for over twenty years.

But Michael also likes the feel of a string tied to a hook on one end and a reel on the other. Like life, fishing too has it's mountain tops and valleys as this musician can attest to. His "high" place in fishing happened when he took a once in a lifetime trip with his dad to the Great Slave Lake in the Northwest territory. Being the only "big time" fly-in fishing trip he and his father went on was pretty special, and the fish did their part to help as they tackled Lake trout, Grayling and Walleye.

At night the warm cabin sheltered them from the spring's cold air, under clear and star filled Canadian skies. Yet, this mountain top time would have one low spot - well almost! One of those cold, clear nights Michael was out and using surface lures, hoping for a big fish to attack. Michael begins, "As a fly fisherman I'm sort of embarrassed to admit this, but we were spin fishing and using those big Hula Poppers that make all kinds of noise on top of the water. That night, all of a sudden I got this unbelievable strike and was convinced it was going to be a good fish. I was reeling it in and reeling it in, and noticed - I was reeling up! A Great Horned owl had picked up the plug from the waters surface and was now sitting high in a tree with my lure! Thankfully - thank the Lord, he didn't get hooked. I don't know how he kept from not getting hooked!" The owl figured out that big old plastic bait was not the dinner he had hoped and worked for, so he dropped it in the tree top and flew away. Snagged in the branches way up there, Michael could not free it so he lost his Hula Popper when the line broke. In conclusion, Michael adds, "It was an interesting way to lose a lure."

It might seem like an accident that a no count Great Horned owl crossed paths with someone whose dream once was to count birds, but nothing happens by chance, not even a sparrow falling from the sky. Michael Card has a peace with God that is eternal, and you can have this peace too! To receive a free booklet on the subject, call, e-mail, or write to us here at God's Great Outdoors and we'll send a copy of "More Than Winning & Losing," by Hank Parker. Plus, you will also receive a copy of "The Ultimate Fishing Challenge," by Jim Grassi.

HERE'S A:
"MY BIGGEST HUNTING BLUNDER" FROM
"God's Great Outdoors"
#003

The president of *Rightnour Manufacturing Company*, Bob Rightnour, gives the business one hundred percent when he's on board at his job. The employees machine precision pieces for use in the medical field. However, this division of *Rightnour Manufacturing* is an off shoot of the company's original production line. That line is as a maker of black powder hunting and shooting accessories. They manufacture over 500 different products for the shooting sports and *Rightnour* distributes a number of other outdoor products as well. With all this knowledge, it's no surprise to find out Bob Rightnour is an avid outdoorsman. And despite the fact he's steeped in black powder product production, the bow and center fire rifle come off the wall in pursuit of big game as well. Plus Pennsylvania, his state of residence, has some homegrown trophies to cause even the hardest driving company president to slip out of the office. Bob being no exception.

Bob Rightnour's blunders are growing as his years afield increase, but twice doing what the experts say you shouldn't, has yielded a prize. So, two of Bob's blunders are really pseudo-blunders and both revolve around black bear.

The first black bear Bob harvested was on a very cold November day. In fact, the temperature was cutting to the bone when Bob decided to head back to the car for a cup of coffee. As he rounded a bend in the laurel covered mountains, he came face to face with a bruin. When Bob squeezed the trigger on his 30-06, he had his first black bear.

Bob tries to pick the highest, most rugged mountains near his Centre County, Pennsylvania home. That's where his second bear came from, a real tough place to access. Bob had hiked a half a mile over a ridge top down through a laurel thicket. Three hundred yards from the top, the tangle of laurels opened up to a nice flat where one could sit and look for considerable distance. That's just what Bob did as he planted himself on a stump. The trouble was it had been raining through the night and had not stopped. It wasn't pouring, but it wasn't a drizzle either. Compounded with the walk through the laurels, Bob was soaked to the skin. Soon the only thing warm on him was his backside, as he sat on a Hot Seat seat cushion; after forty-five minutes of this cold and wet condition, Bob was ready to jump at the chance to move. So, when a party of seven hunters arrived at the ridge top to drive the area, he stood up to go. Something caught his eye and Bob turned to see a bear only fifteen paces away. He had no time to get scared as he aimed his gun, finding a scope full of nothing but black hair. Bob remembers, "It happened so fast, I had time to do nothing but react!" Pointing the rifle where it needed to go ended the matter. Bob feels the bear came out of the laurels where he'd walked, but the wet conditions hid his scent. He had traveled through the wet tangle as not to leave a scent trail on the flat where he expected the bear to come from.

Bob Rightnour's cold conditions which caused him to move may have turned for good on his bear hunts, but Bob did not leave his eternal future to blind luck. Fact is, any time is the right time, so he's made eternal life sure in Jesus Christ and you can too. To receive a free booklet on the subject called "The Ultimate Hunt," by Charlie Alsheimer, contact us here at God's Great Outdoors by phone, mail, or e-mail. You will also get Dwight Schuh's "The Greatest Hunt of All."

"A War Of Wits"
#003

As a Civil War general, lawyer, author, and governor of the New Mexico Territory, Lew Wallace was not a religious man; though he knew a number of Bible stories. When he met Col. Robert G. Ingersoll, he asked this famous agnostic of his beliefs about God and life eternal. For two hours, Ingersoll argued his negative position on such matters, and oddly, the conversation sent Lew Wallace into a spiritual tug-of-war about what was true. On parting, the unbeliever challenged the non-believer to prove Jesus Christ was the Son of God. Wallace needed the arguments of an agnostic to cause him to investigate the truth.

The book, Ben-Hur is the result of Wallace's tireless and extensive research. Writing this novel took seven years, and Wallace is remembered as saying the writing of, Ben-Hur led to his accepting Jesus Christ as Lord of his life.

Later, while serving as the United States Minister to the Ottoman Empire in Constantinople, he was able to take a trip to The Holy Land. He discovered how his research in the writing of, Ben-Hur had been exact in every detail. The funny thing is, in 1880 when Lew Wallace finished his famous novel, only a fraction of the evidence of the Bible's proof known today was available to him then. Yet there was enough to guide him to the truth.

Psalm 119:105
"Your word is a lamp to my feet and a light for my path."

Day Four

HERE'S A: "ONE THAT GOT AWAY" FISHING STORY FROM
"God's Great Outdoors"
#004

The fishing adventure John Storm would most like to forget, took place in-and-out of a bass boat on Oklahoma's Lake Texoma. Back then, John's job was in the marketing area of the family owned business which began in 1964 with their original release, "The Thin Fin" fishing lure. While his job at *Storm Lures* had him more on the road than on the lake, that fateful day found him throwing top water baits around boat docks. When his "Chug Bug" hung up on one of the structures, the only thing to do was aim the trolling motor in the direction of the snagged lure to retrieve it. It's true, even people who work at a fishing tackle company go after lures after their casts go amiss.

John remembers, "The docks there have Styrofoam underneath and usually they've got that square-shaped structure (metal) to hold the Styrofoam. Being the smart person that I am, I left one foot on the edge of the boat and the other foot on the Styrofoam. Little did I know that the Styrofoam wasn't attached. So the Styrofoam goes straight down." John's leg went under water as soon as he put weight on the Styrofoam square. Losing his balance and being attached to his sinking leg, John's body decided to join in on the descent to the lake's bottom, which created a very large splash, as you might imagine. Fighting the inevitable forces of gravity, John scraped the "fire out of his leg" on the metal structure on the dock. Then he swung his arm around and smashed it into the dock's wood and tore off four inches of flesh. Both John's eyeglasses and fishing pole followed his descent, and to top it off, his Christian brother in the boat's stern rubbed salt in to the wound with the comment of, "Cool move, nice watch"— "Your watch! Your watch!" So, John threw his arm "bleeding like crazy" above his head to keep his new watch above water. After recovering from the shock of the whole ordeal and removing his watch, John spent the next twenty minutes diving 8 feet down in chilly autumn water to search for and recover his glasses and rod. John reflects, "I wish it was one of those experiences I had on video tape, 'cause I could have made a million dollars off of that good blooper."

John Storm may have gone down in that fishing misadventure, but one place he has his footing solidly placed, is when it comes to life ever after. You can also find a rock solid foundation and it is in Christ Jesus. To know more, write, call, or e-mail us here at God's Great Outdoors and ask to receive Hank Parker's booklet called, "More Than Winning and Losing." It is yours free! And comes with "The Ultimate Fishing Challenge," by Jim Grassi.

HERE'S A:
"MY BIGGEST HUNTING BLUNDER" FROM
"God's Great Outdoors"
Adapted From Steve Chapman's Book, *A LOOK AT LIFE FROM A DEER STAND*
Edited For Radio Broadcast By Gerry Caillouet
#004

Most weekends find Steve and Annie Chapman ministering in concert some-where across the North American continent, but come Monday when the Chapmans fly home, if the hunting season is in Steve is out trying to persuade a big buck to come home and be potluck; supper that is. Well things don't always go as planned. Join us as we share what Steve Chapman calls "The Bladder Blunder."

"As far as blunders go, for every hunter (including me) it's not *if* something will go wrong, it's <u>when</u> will it happen. I've had my share, but I must say my greatest blunder is one single frustrating thing that seems to reoccur. Far too often." adds Steve.

"My first disappointing experience with this blunder came early in my hunting life. It was during one of my first few deer hunts. I was a teenager and was going out on a bitter cold morning in West Virginia. At that age I had a raging appetite, so before my friend picked me up I had to have some breakfast. I made myself a bowl of cereal and milk. You must understand, a bowl of cereal for a "growing boy" is not just a bite and swallow. I ate my cereal out of a 3 pound washtub. This required of course, about a half gallon of milk.

"I had my breakfast and headed off to the woods. I sat for around two hours on the ice cold ground. Sure enough, you guessed it, the milk caught up with me. My bladder began to swell to the size of a basketball. I tried not to think about it, but I had no success. I couldn't take it any longer. I yielded to the pain.

"As you can also guess, at the very moment I, how shall I say it, began to experience relief, here came the deer. Running right up to within 20 yards of me, we both were surprised. It never fails. With my 30-30 out of reach I said good-by to the deer as it bounded off to another county. How many times has this happened to me? Too many to tell about. It hasn't always been a bladder blunder, however. Sometimes it's been simple impatience that has messed me up. Yet, what wonderful opportunities to learn endurance and patience that hunting has yielded."

Now, Steve Chapman may have missed the mark on that hunt, but one hunting trip he didn't miss out on was the hunt for eternal life through Jesus Christ. You also can find success in the ultimate of hunts, the one for eternal salvation.

For a free booklet by Charlie Alsheimer entitled "The Ultimate Hunt," contact God's Great Outdoors by mail, phone, or e-mail and we'll be glad to send you one along with a free copy of "The Greatest Hunt of All," by Dwight Schuh.

"The Scales of Truth and Justice"
#004

It's a well-known fact, "Organized religion is a sham and a crutch for weak-minded people who need strength in numbers." Even the governor of an upper Midwest state where adults sprout horns, paint faces, and clad their bodies in purple every autumn, knows it. What this public servant of this land with ten thousand lakes does not know is a personal relationship with Jesus Christ is not a religion, it is a life-changing experience.

Lee Strobel, an award-winning journalist who served on the *Chicago Tribune,* was a spiritual skeptic. When his fun and adventurous wife Leslie announced that she had become a Christian, Lee expected trouble. However, he was both pleasantly surprised and fascinated by the shift in Leslie's character. These changes sparked a desire to examine what the source of the subtle, but significant changes in his wife's attitude were from. Thus began the investigative reporter's search of all the available evidence of Jesus Christ and the Bible. He plunged into his study with more energy than any crime scene or study he had ever worked on. Setting aside any prejudices, he read books, analyzed history, interviewed experts, examined archaeology, ancient literature, and for the first time, read God's word verse by verse.

In the end, Lee Strobell, the recipient of a Master's of Studies in Law from Yale School of Law, followed his wife Leslie in becoming a Christian. His extensive study is available to help you disprove the Bible on your path to worldly fame and fortune. You see, Lee Strobel's book *The Case For Christ* (Zondervan Publishing House) also lists all those authorities who disbelieve in the Bible. So, you do not have to hunt the critics you will need for your research. Who could ask for anything more? Just be reminded, the scales tip both ways, as Lee Strobel discovered.

2 Timothy 3:16
"All Scripture is God-breathed and is useful for teaching, rebuking, correcting, and training in righteousness,"

Day Five
HERE'S A: "ONE THAT GOT AWAY" FISHING STORY FROM
"God's Great Outdoors"
#005

An *Orvis* endorsed fly fishing instructor and guide, Dick Hribar, (re-bar) has also loved to canoe all his life. That love was kindled by his father, who taught Dick the proper ways to handle a canoe. Top on his dad's list, was safety. Only once did Dick shy away from honoring his father's lessons in canoeing safety and it almost cost him and his spouse their lives.

Preparing to take his wife with him on her first ever canoe trip, Dick decided to have his young bride accompany him to a local beaver pond. It was the evening before they would be leaving with the others in the trail club to which Dick was a member of. The April air was cool and water temperature was in the forties. Trying to be nice, he placed a small stump in the canoe for his wife to sit on. This was his first mistake, and his father being the man of sense and safety he was had taught him to always kneel on a canoe's floor to keep the center of gravity low.

Dick says, "If that wasn't dumb enough, I for some reason had hip boots on. Something my Pop always preached against while in a canoe." Well, the two paddled out and Dick began instructing on the way to paddle the water craft. When his novice mate began paddling on the same side as Dick, the canoe started to lean, and over it went, spilling them under the pond's surface. The water was so cold it took their breath away. Thus, Dick was unable to tell his wife what to do and his hip boots were now full of water pulling him down. Thank God Dick had not hooked the boots to his belt, so he worked to pull first one, and then the other hip boot off. With the weight of the boots gone, he helped his wife to the shore and safety.

Now Dick Hribar may have acted unsafe when it comes to canoeing, but Dick is safe in looking toward the life he'll live in the hereafter. If you also want to have the peace of a safe journey into the next life, a life at peace with Jesus Christ, call, write, or e-mail us here at God's Great Outdoors and we'll send you the free booklet by Hank Parker called, "More Than Winning and Losing." We will also mail you "The Ultimate Fishing Challenge," by Jim Grassi.

HERE'S A:
"MY BIGGEST HUNTING BLUNDER" FROM
"God's Great Outdoors"
#005

M.R. James, the Founder/Editor In Chief of BOWHUNTER Magazine, admits he's had his share of hunting blunders during the past four decades. He says, "Many people think because I work for a bowhunting magazine, I'll always get game. Well, that, simply not the case."

One mule deer bowhunt that took place over 25 years ago is a perfect example of one hunting blunder that left M.R. a bit red-faced. He was in Utah's Book Cliffs on the famed Tavaputs Plateau Ranch still-hunting among sage-covered hills and shady groves of quaking aspen. The weather was typical for late August - cool mornings and warm days - making for good summertime deer hunting action.

While afield one day M.R. encountered two other deer hunters staying at the same ranch lodge. One of the bowhunters had just arrowed a fine buck and he and his partner were busy field dressing the muley when M.R. came on the scene, offered his congratulations and paused long enough to hear the details of the successful shot. As the three men stood talking, they suddenly fell silent when they heard the unmistakable thump-thump-thump of mule deer bounding their way down a timbered ridge. Seconds later a velvet-racked muley appeared and slid to a surprised stop less than 15 yards from the trio of camouflaged bowhunters. M.R., who was holding his recurve bow, immediately nocked an arrow, drew and shot - right under the broadside buck's chest! The lucky deer quickly departed for parts unknown, leaving one very embarrassed hunter and two eyewitnesses watching him bounce away and disappear into the trees.

At this point the two hunters exchanged a knowing look. Then one of them turned to M.R., smiled and asked, "You say you write for a bowhunting magazine?"

Well, M.R. James may have under shot that mule deer buck, but his aim isn't always off. In fact, when it comes to eternal life there's no second chance like sometimes might happen in bowhunting. M.R. has scored forever, by placing his trust in Jesus Christ as Lord and Savior. You can also have the peace of eternal life in Jesus. For a free booklet on the subject, write, phone, or e-mail God's Great Outdoors for your free copy of "The Ultimate Hunt," by Charlie Alsheimer. You will also be sent Dwight Schuh's "The Greatest Hunt of All."

"It All Adds Up"
#005

One of the most creative and inventive people I've ever had the privilege to interview is Matt McPherson. Yet, despite his roots in archery both in recreation and the business world, the first time I interviewed Matt, he wanted to talk about the Bible and a video project he'd recently worked on. Matt was the Executive Producer of an award-winning video titled, *Secrets of the Bible Code Revealed.* (Grizzly Adams Productions, Inc.)

The Bible Code has nothing to do with numerology, theomatics or gematria. It is an encrypted code found within the Hebrew text of the Bible, revealing future events in history that could have only been known by God at the time the Bible was written. These are the same type of codes used by the Germans and Japanese in World War II, and are still used today. Yet, only because of today's advanced computers could this have been uncovered.

This equal distanced letter sequence or ELS Code was first tested on computer by the famous Jewish mathematician, Dr. Ripps. His findings were sent to the mathematical journal, *Statistical Science* which publishes nothing until it's thoroughly tested. The tests that were run supported Dr. Ripps' finding. When Harold Gans, the Senior Cryptologist/Mathematician for the National Security Agency, read the findings in *Statistical Science*, he decided to check the probability that these codes could appear by accident. His computer program came up with P=0.0004637 or the probability of it being an accident as virtually non-existent.

Can the Bible stand on it's own without a code hidden within the original Hebrew text? Yes! But, perhaps a loving God, knowing a day would come when some intellectual minds would need a computer-age discovery that adds even more greatness to an already awesome God, that He loved them so much he revealed himself in this way to all, so that some might be saved and live with him for eternity.

Isaiah 40:13
"Who has understood the mind of the Lord, or instructed him as his counselor?"

Day Six
HERE'S A: "ONE THAT GOT AWAY"
FISHING STORY FROM
"God's Great Outdoors"
#006

In 1964, Homer Circle became the Special Features Writer of *Sports Afield* magazine. Now in his eighties, Uncle Homer's stories have appeared in this monthly outdoor magazine for thirty-five years

As a boy, Homer would carve "Little Crab," (as he called them), fishing plugs out of old walnut blocks which worked quite well on the southern Ohio fish. A few years later he was writing angling articles for a Springfield, Ohio paper when he decided to try to sell his "Little Crab" lure to a fishing tackle manufacturer. Instead they decided to hire him. His writing continued as well and the tips he shared have carried him to remote fishing spots around the world. But the fishing adventure that almost cost him his life happened near Dowagiac, Michigan. Homer was in the mood for some trout and Dowagiac (Do-Wa-Jack) Creek seemed like the place to satisfy his cravings. But as he began to cross a small stream in order to get to the other side, he became stuck in the middle. The mucky bottom was sucking him in deeper the more he struggled to get out. Soon the water was coming in over his waders and what started as just a nuisance was now turning very serious. Homer said, "The harder I struggled, the deeper in I became." With the water to his chest and then shoulders, he realized the hole he was in was real trouble.

"All of a sudden, as if a light shone down, I felt this sort of lift," reflects Homer. "I looked over and saw this root five feet away. I turned my fly rod around and dropped the reel over that root and slowly and laboriously pulled myself out of the muck onto the bank."

Homers' waders were filled with water and the smelly mud he'd been sinking in. Removing them he surveyed himself, he was a mess. Homer, thinking out loud said, "Go on home, it wasn't your day."

That isn't the only pit Homer has escaped from in his life. When Homer asked Jesus Christ to be his Lord and Savior, Homer escaped the pit of everlasting fire reserved for Satan and his followers, the fallen angels. You also can find assurance that you'll never be in that pit. To find out more, call, write, or e-mail us here at God's Great Outdoors and we'll send you a free booklet by Hank Parker called, "More Than Winning and Losing." Along with this booklet you will also receive "The Ultimate Fishing Challenge," by Jim Grassi.

HERE'S A:
"MY BIGGEST HUNTING BLUNDER" FROM
"God's Great Outdoors"
Adapted From Dwight Schuh's Book, *HUNTING OPEN-COUNTRY MULE DEER*
Edited For Radio Broadcast By Gerry Caillouet
#006

The Editor of BOWHUNTER Magazine, Dwight Schuh, warns mule deer hunters not to give up too soon. In his book, *Hunting Open-Country Mule Deer*, Dwight reflects on one time that he did just that. It was an indelible lesson. Dwight recalls, "I was hunting Oregon's Blue Mountains on a blustery day in September. Occasionally, rays of sun stabbed through the black clouds with gentle warmth, but mostly the clouds won out. Perched on the south side of a jagged canyon looking north, I spotted a decent four point."

Dwight said to himself, "Ah, man! Look at that nice buck. That's the one for me. About that time a massive set of antlers rose from the plum bushes behind the first buck," continues Dwight. "They reminded me of moose antlers, so grossly did they dwarf the other buck's rack. I quickly set up the spotting scope and stared. Never had I seen such an animal! I'd crawl to the moon for a buck like that. He was and still is the biggest buck I've ever seen."

Dwight studied the animal and landscape. Then, the stalk was on. "The wind whipped this way and that, and it seemed sure the bucks would smell me. To add further doubt, when I got on the bucks' side, the layout wasn't so clear. There were several plum patches, and I couldn't be sure where the deer had been. As I hunkered under a tree waiting for a seething snow storm to blow by, I felt sure I'd come to the right patch, but there was no way of knowing for sure, and I couldn't see any sign of the deer.

"About that time, a grouse jumped up on a rock 15 feet away, clucking, tempting me. I was freezing and hungry, and roast grouse seemed like just what the doctor would order under such conditions." With the wind swirling, Dwight thought surely the deer had smelled him. And he wasn't sure he was even at the right location. Convincing himself the bucks were gone, Dwight shot a blunt-point arrow at his future dinner. Missing the grouse, the arrow clanged off the rock. Laments Dwight, "A sickening explosion took place in the nearest plum bushes. Huge antlers erupted 20 yards away as the bucks sprang to their feet and vacated."

Dwight may have missed out on that hunt, but one hunting trip he didn't miss out on was the hunt for eternal life through Jesus Christ. You also can find success in the ultimate of hunts, the one for eternal salvation. If you would like to know how, let God's Great Outdoors know and we will send you a free booklet by Charlie Alsheimer entitled, "The Ultimate Hunt." And we will also send you "The Greatest Hunt of All" by Dwight Schuh, too!

"Where's The Beef?"
#006

If you know anything about history, you are aware of the fact that the Bible has many times been the subject of governmental attacks. Why? If the Bible is just a book of history or sets down some basic principles for living that one doesn't really need to apply anyway, what's the fuss? Could it be that this book states things that so convict people of their sinfulness and the future consequences of this sinful condition that they feel forced to act with anger?

In 1384 when John Wycliffe became the first person to translate the Bible into

English, he was executed. Then from 1484-1536 William Tyndale printed Bibles to place in the hands of every Englishman, from commoner to king. He was burned at the stake. There must be something special about the Bible, as the writings of Shakespeare have never stirred up such action that I know of.

Then explain this one, in the 1930's Joseph Stalin ordered all Bibles confiscated and Stavropol, Russia was no exception. This city's Bibles were stored over sixty years in a warehouse outside of town until the early 1990's. It was at this time as *CoMission* members worked in this area of Russia that they asked officials if they could have the Bibles to distribute in their evangelistic efforts. When they were given permission, the *CoMission* members arrived the next day at the warehouse with a truck and several hired Russian helpers. One was a young man who as an agnostic and skeptic, talked against their efforts, being only there for the money. Later a team member noticed this young antagonists' disappearance and began looking for him. The Russian had taken a Bible to hide for himself and opened the book to the inside page. When the *CoMission* worker found him he was weeping because there he had found his own grandmother's signature. It was her Bible, a woman persecuted all her life for her faith. Among all those thousands of Bibles, her grandson had stolen the one book that could have suddenly ripped open his heart to the redemptive power of God's holy word.

Acts 16:31
"They replied, 'Believe in the Lord Jesus, and you will be saved — you and your household.'"

Day Seven

HERE'S A: "ONE THAT GOT AWAY" FISHING STORY FROM
"God's Great Outdoors"
#007

Daryl Christensen has been a pro Walleye fisherman for many years now, fishing on both the *In-Fisherman* and *Cabela's* Walleye Trails: he's chalked-up quite a few years of professional fishing experience. Some, as you'll see was learned the hard way.

Daryl's story will really shock you, but not as much as it did him. It happened in June, several years ago. He and an amateur fisherman were fishing a pro-am tournament on Minnesota's Mille Lacs Lake. Fishing six miles off shore, he and his amateur fishing partner had finally found a "honey hole" and the fish were coming aboard as quickly as they could set the hook.

Unfortunately, a thunder head was making it's way across the lake heading right over them. These were the days before Loranes or GPS's, so Daryl was not sure they could find the spot again if they pulled anchor and headed for safety. Daryl had stayed out in similar situations before, so he opted to test this one. As the dark clouds rumbled closer, Daryl joked, "I'm ready if God wants me." "Well, I'm not!," was the amateur's reply. A few minutes later he made the statement to his fishing partner, "If the next strike passes, we're in the clear." As he finished the last word in the sentence, a bolt hit Daryl's 8 ½ foot graphite rod. The charge went down the rod into the boat, knocking Daryl over. Daryl asked his amateur partner if he knew CPR, "No." was his reply. Daryl's statement to this was, "I guess I'm going to die," then he passed out for a couple of minutes. When Daryl came to he climbed into the seat and began fishing. Totally shocked by all this, the amateur tried to talk him into going in for medical treatment. Daryl refused and fished on, between being sick and passing out. After three hours went by, he started to return to his normal self. About the incident, Daryl says, "I'd gotten away with it so many times, it was bound to happen." Now he doesn't take chances like that anymore.

Had Daryl been killed by that lightning bolt, because he had previously asked Jesus Christ to be his Lord and Savior, he would have gone straight to Heaven. As unthinking as it might have been to stay on in the storm, it is a mistake far greater to not find peace with God. In fact, it is an eternal mistake.

For a free booklet on the subject by Hank Parker, contact us here at God's Great Outdoors by mail, phone, or e-mail and we will send you a copy of "More Than Winning and Losing," and "The Ultimate Fishing Challenge," by Jim Grassi.

HERE'S A:
"MY BIGGEST HUNTING BLUNDER" FROM
"God's Great Outdoors"
Written By Dr. Tom Rakow And Edited For Radio Broadcast By Gerry Caillouet
#007

The Founder and Executive President of *The Christian Deer Hunters Association*, Dr. Tom Rakow, remembers the onset of a non-fatal disease that is not uncommon among deer hunters.

"I will long remember the opening day of my very first deer season," says Tom. "A member of our hunting party kicked out a nice six-pointer to me which stopped broadside only yards away. You could not have asked for an easier shot. Unfortunately, I fell under the influence of 'buck fever.'

"I had heard that 'buck fever' was famous for making hunters behave in some strange ways. It made them do things like: shout 'bang! bang!' and never fire a shot, or lever unfired rounds on the ground. I even remember reading of one hunter who received two broken legs as well. In all the excitement he forgot he was in a treestand more than fifteen feet off of the ground!

"For me 'buck fever' meant having arms that felt like lead. I knew what I wanted to do. I knew what I needed to do. But, for some strange reason I just couldn't bring the rifle to my shoulder. Instead, I shot eight times from the hip hitting dirt and trees just a few feet in front of me. I watched helplessly as the buck finally bounded out of sight. This was my initial and (hopefully) most memorable experience with a severe case of the jitters commonly known as 'buck fever.' "

Nevertheless, as powerful as "buck fever" may seem there is a force far stronger at work in our lives. It's an energy that frequently explodes and injures everyone who it comes in contact with it. This negative force is known as the "sin nature". It was this same power that caused the apostle Paul to say at one point, "...when I want to do good, evil is right there with me." (Romans 7:21)

However, God has not left us helpless. He has provided a "helper." There is someone who will take up residence in our life and begin bringing our sinful nature under control. The name of this helper is the Holy Spirit.

If we have truly trusted Jesus Christ as our Savior, the Holy Spirit dwells inside of us and seeks to help us live lives that are pleasing to the Lord. As the apostle Paul reminded the Believers in Rome, "You, however, are controlled not by the sinful nature but by the Spirit, if the Spirit of God lives in you. And if anyone does not have the Spirit of Christ, he does not belong to Christ." (Romans 8:9)

Tom may have missed the mark on that hunt, but one hunting trip he didn't miss out on, the hunt for eternal life through Jesus Christ. You also can find success in the ultimate of hunts, the one for eternal salvation. If you would like to know more about finding eternal salvation, contact us here at God's Great Outdoors by mail, phone, or e-mail and we will send you a free booklet by Charlie Alsheimer called, "The Ultimate Hunt." With it you'll get "The Greatest Hunt of All" by Dwight Schuh.

"Round 1"
#007

What on earth could generate such anger and hatred for a book, the Bible, and those who proclaim the message hidden within it's pages? Nothing on earth we can see, but there is a being who roams freely, looking to destroy everything and everyone that would keep him from his goal, which is to set himself above God in Heaven.

As a young man, I did not know if there was a God. But, I was sure there must be a devil. I could see evil and it's effects all around me. Jesus, I knew existed historically, but was he the Son of God? And why was this spiritual enemy, Satan, trying to oppose him if he was the Messiah and the Prince of Peace?

Lucifer, the Morning Star, was the highest ranking angel God created. But this powerful spiritual being was not satisfied with his position and tried to place himself above the very One who made him. Because of his rebellion, Satan and those angels who followed in the failed coup were forced to leave their Heavenly realm and so made war on one of God's creations, man. Humans are made in the image and likeness of God. But, understand, Satan is not just fighting for the souls of men because he is out for vengeance, "an eye for an eye" so to speak. Satan's goal is still the same as from the beginning - to defeat God anyway he can and if that means destroying some or all of mankind, on the way to his attempt at victory, that is what this enemy of God and his demonic force will do.

1 Peter 5:8
"Be self-controlled and alert. Your enemy the devil prowls around like a roaring lion looking for someone to devour."

Day Eight
HERE'S A: "ONE THAT GOT AWAY"
FISHING STORY FROM
"God's Great Outdoors"
#008

The director of marketing for the *Zebco Company*, Gary Dollahon (dall-a-hon) was fishing with two close friends on Lake Powell. That afternoon in late October, the threesome had gotten into a school of Stripers, and stayed with them till sunset. That was a mistake that would almost cost them their lives.

You see, Lake Powell is huge and the men had almost a thirty-five mile run to the southern part where they were camped. As they headed back, the winds got up to 35 mph out of the south. This concerned them all as the lake's water level was low, creating new uncharted islands that were no longer underwater and hard to see. Finally, they reached the one last, long stretch of islands. It was difficult to see if their boat was in the last curve just before they turned to go to the marina which was almost a mile and a half away.

Going along with a spotlight, they had just glimpsed the marina lights across the island. This told them that the boat had cleared and the three knew they now had a straight shot in, when trouble really began. Gary remembers, "I had just uttered the words, 'Well we've got it made now because we've passed the island,' when all of a sudden the boat struck a six foot steel marker buoy that was in the channel." Even with the slow speed, the collision caused the boat to go sideways enough to let waves come up over the side, filling the boat and killing the motor.

Totally submerged with the gunwales at the top of water level, the crew worked frantically to put on life jackets. But before they could, the boat grounded on the same island they had just worked so hard to get by. The vessel continued to be filled with water as the winds whipped wave after wave at them. The late October air temperature in that Utah and Arizona border location they were now ship-wrecked in was forty-five degrees.

Gary started feeling the effects of the chilly wind and water immediately as hypothermia set in. He got out and took shelter behind a huge rock to get out of the wind. Gary reflects, "As I was laying there, I remembered looking up and seeing a full moon just coming up on the horizon and thinking to myself, 'Boy I'm really in the hands of the Good Lord now,' and I started thinking about my wife and daughter. Got to thinking about what kind of life they would have without me, and the next thing I knew I heard someone calling my name. I looked back up at the moon and the moon was much higher in the sky, so I had actually passed out or gone to sleep, or whatever. But the voice was coming from one of the two fishermen who was saying, 'Gary come on, we've got a fire.' "

Where did they get the wood on that sandy island, Gary wondered? Tumbleweeds! A huge pile of tumbleweeds and the fire felt great. They spent the rest of the night picking up and burning tumbleweeds. This kept them busy and warm till first light, when the boat traffic started and they were spotted on the island as they flashed to the passing vessels with a signal mirror pulled from the boat's emergency kit.

The dawn also shed light on the fact that Gary had taken shelter behind the only rock on that entire island! But it is not the only rock in which Gary Dollahon has found rest. He has also placed his trust on the Solid Rock, Christ Jesus and so he knows his eternity is with Him forever, and you can too! Contact us here at God's Great Outdoors by mail, phone, or e-mail to receive a free booklet by Hank Parker called, "More Than Winning & Losing.". Plus, we'll also send you "The Ultimate Fishing Challenge," by Jim Grassi.

HERE'S A:
"MY BIGGEST HUNTING BLUNDER" FROM
"God's Great Outdoors"
Written By Larry D. Jones And Edited For Radio Broadcast By Gerry Caillouet
#008

As President of *Wilderness Sound Productions*, and one of the West's well-known bowhunters, Larry D. Jones remembers how he goofed up while hunting turkey in Northern California with two friends, Dwight Schuh (shoe), and Cliff Dewell (duel).

"On this hunt, I decided to hunt with a shotgun first, and use my bow to hunt a second bird," Larry recalls. "Cliff had volunteered to do the calling, so I suggested Dwight take the first shot since he was hunting with his bow, then I'd try to get an opportunity with my shotgun."

"After an hour of roving and calling, a gobbler answered, so we set-up. Dwight settled in the shadows on the right, I crouched in the bushes to the left, while Cliff crept 20 yards behind and began to call."

"Two toms strutted toward us, side-by-side. I settled my sights on the left bird's head assuming Dwight would take the bird on the right."

"All I could see was the gobbler's head because of brush, so instantly after I heard Dwight's shot, the bird sprang upward. I assumed Dwight had shot low, so as the gobbler came down, I squeezed the trigger. The bird dropped like a lead balloon. Dwight and I ran forward. I was dumbfounded when I found Dwight's arrow, crumpled and pelted with lead shot, imbedded in the bird's chest."

"I felt terrible, but Dwight being a good friend, quickly understood my mistake and forgave me. We hunted on, and an hour later, I had my bird."

"My blunder continued. A few months later Dwight's wife, Laura, invited friends to celebrate Dwight's birthday. She decided to serve wild turkey. Prior to

34

dinner, Dwight mentioned he had harvested the turkey with his bow. Later as friends chomped on lead shot, I'm sure he had to wonder why he hunts with me."

Larry may have fouled up by targeting the same bird as his good friend Dwight, but there is another hunt Larry scored big on, that is the hunt for eternal life through Jesus Christ. You too can find success in the ultimate of hunts, the one for eternal salvation. To be successful in the same way, contact God's Great Outdoors by mail, phone, or e-mail for a free booklet by Charlie Alsheimer, entitled "The Ultimate Hunt." We will also mail you a copy of "The Greatest Hunt of All," written by Dwight Schuh.

"Sour Puss"
#008

Have you ever heard someone say, "I bet Satan laughed over that!"? They were perhaps talking of someone and the sin in their lives that caused a family to breakup or a church to split. The consequences of sin, the end results may look like the enemy is winning, but it is just one battle in the war between the forces of evil and Almighty God.

I don't believe Satan laughs, he knows the "Rest of the story," as Paul Harvey would say. Satan and his army of followers were present when the events in the Bible happened. Fact is, they were working to destroy God's plan of redemption all along the way. This band of desperados acted to prevent the writing of the original manuscript. Then the fallen angels tried to prevent the masses from reading the Bible or owning a copy of their very own. Why? Because the word of God changes lives through the supernatural power of the Holy Spirit, and changed lives accomplish God's work bringing about God's plan and verifying the validity of God's word.

So, Satan and his demons are working feverishly to destroy what God's word says. If they can cause one line of the Holy Bible to be a lie, then the Creator God, who authored the infallible word of God, would have orchestrated a book that was imperfect. But try as hard as this demonic foe may, it is just not going to happen!

James 1:13-15
"When tempted, no one should say, 'God is tempting me.' For God cannot be tempted by evil, nor does he tempt anyone; but each one is tempted when, by his own evil desire, he is dragged away and enticed. Then, after desire has conceived, it gives birth to sin; and sin, when it is full-grown, gives birth to death."

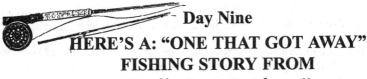

Day Nine

HERE'S A: "ONE THAT GOT AWAY" FISHING STORY FROM
"God's Great Outdoors"

#009

Written By Ken Reed And Edited For Radio Broadcast By Gerry Caillouet

For the owner of **Blu-Dun** *Taxidermy And Guide Service*, remote trout ponds offer great fishing in the state of Maine, and the only way to get to these "Jewels of the Mountains" is by foot, walking that is. Ken Reed is a taxidermist and professional hunting and fishing guide by trade. Despite his professionalism, even this Maine woodsman can get a little "froggy."

Ken begins, "Last summer after hiking into one of my favorite ponds, my client and I blew up the belly boats, rigged up the fly rods, and had a fine morning of trout fishing. Around one o'clock I kicked my way back to shore, climbed out of the belly boat, and started the lunch fire.

"Thick strip steaks, marinated mushrooms, and coleslaw was the fare. My client climbed ashore as the aroma of the steaks cooking over the open fire filled the lake valley. He was impressed by the succulent steaks and was hungry after the long hike and morning of fishing.

"Paul was a doctor from Maryland, and this was his first fishing trip with me as his guide. I was busy looking for utensils and plates, when it dawned on me!....the plates were two miles away in the back of my pick-up truck.

"Oh, no! Those big juicy steaks were done, and nowhere to put them. The only flat surface available was the kick fins, used to propel the belly boat and so it was, steak and mushrooms on a fin.

"I'm sure it was a first; like eating off of a giant frog's foot. The steaks were tender and the afternoon weather front cooperated. Praise the Lord for even those times when the best of plans fold, and the fish make up for it."

Well, Ken Reed may have forgotten some of his needs that time, but there is one thing Ken did remember. That's to gain peace through eternal life in Jesus Christ. You also can be a part of God's ultimate fishing creel and thus be assured of winning out for all eternity. If you would like more information, contact us here by mail, phone, or e-mail at God's Great Outdoors and we would be happy to send you a free copy of the booklet by Hank Parker called, "More Than Winning and Losing." You'll also receive a free copy of the "The Ultimate Fishing Challenge," by Jim Grassi.

HERE'S A:
"MY BIGGEST HUNTING BLUNDER" FROM
"God's Great Outdoors"
#009

The President and Founder of *Christian Bowhunters of America*, David L. Roose, never seems to get serious about hunting deer until late in October. Yet, early one October, Dave and his son decided to hunt the Huron National Forest, which just happens to be right out the back door of his Cadillac, Michigan home.

When his son, Paul, opted to take the spot Dave generally hunts, Dave settled on a tree stand in a location he knew he saw mostly doe activity.

As he headed to his stand site for the evening hunt, Dave broke from his tradition of not walking on a known deer trail. Dave later remembered, "I did something I never do. I walked a short distance down the deer trail to the tree my stand was in. I never do this," Dave repeated, "Never!" Later, Dave, who wasn't expecting to see any deer, was called back to reality as movement to his left caught his eye. Dave was awe struck! There, the largest racked buck this seasoned bowhunter had ever seen was coming down the trail he had just walked on. "At the very spot I had stepped onto the deer trail, the buck came to full alert and slammed on the brakes. I could see the deer's every muscle tighten." Dave said. The deer began looking, carefully searching to find the source of what he knew had walked "his" trail.

"I don't like shooting from a sitting position," adds Dave. "But, I dared not attempt standing. Moving my bow slowly, this way and that, I couldn't get to where I could come to full draw and make a good shot." The big buck kept trying to figure things out as Dave tried to draw three times. The third time, Dave's bow tip hit the side of the treestand, the sound reached the buck's ears. The deer blasted sideways and disappeared in some thick balsum firs.

Dave may have lost out on that hunt by stepping in the wrong place, but one path where he's walked that he didn't lose was the hunt for eternal life through Jesus Christ. You also can find success in the ultimate of hunts, the one for eternal salvation. Contact us here at God's Great Outdoors by mail, phone, or e-mail for a free booklet by Charlie Alsheimer called "The Ultimate Hunt." You'll also receive a copy of "The Greatest Hunt of All," by Dwight Schuh.

"Bait & Switch"
#009

It is said that, "A rose by any other word would smell as sweet." This is true of Satan, which by definition means, "adversary." But this enemy of The Living God has many names all of which, when examined, paint a much clearer portrait of his real identity. He is the accuser and the dragon because of his baseness and fierceness. The word "devil" means "slander" and he is called a murderer and a liar. He is the deceiver, who is both "Prince of the World" and of the air. The destroyer, tempter, evil one, and Satan is labeled "the god of this age."

In his course to make God Almighty's plans fail, he and the third of the angels who fell with him have at the hands of wicked sinful men tried to annihilate the Jewish nation time and again. Two cases in point would be the treachery of a man named Haman during the time of captivity by Persia. Then, more recently, a genocide was orchestrated by the leader of the German Nazi Party, Adolf Hitler. With Haman the end of the Jewish people would have meant no family line from which a "Savior of the world" could come. This is because the Messiah was to be of God's chosen people - the nation of Israel.

What of the holocaust during World War II and all the Jews, if they had been removed from the face of the earth? There would have been no nation of Israel to rise up out of the dust of the Middle East, where many years before a mighty people had existed - God's chosen people - Israel. Thus, when the King of Kings returns in the end as God's word prophesies, there would be no Jewish people to cry out in one voice to their Messiah as they then realize who Jesus Christ is - Emmanuel - "God with us." But you see whatever the enemy does, God uses it to achieve His purposes, so try as he might, Satan is doomed to destruction!

Romans 8:28
"And we know that in all things God works for the good of those who love him, who have been called according to his purpose."

Day Ten
HERE'S A: "ONE THAT GOT AWAY"
FISHING STORY FROM
"God's Great Outdoors"
#010

Working hand in hand, Rodger Loomis and his wife Sandy, the owners of The *Attacker Lure Company* and the *Oneida Eagle Bow,* make it a family affair. But this present day joint operation may never have happened had not God's hand intervened in Rodger's life some years before.

Rodger was fishing on Lake Ontario with his good friend and his then two small boys, Brick and Josh. It was a beautiful, sunny afternoon and to top it off the Small Mouth Bass were cooperating fully. The group was catching fish as fast as they could get their line in the water.

Anchored a half mile off shore, or from port, they had the water to themselves. This fact was about to play against their very lives. Suddenly out of the southwest, a violent storm blew in without warning. The high bluffs on shore had hidden the storm's approach until it was upon them. To make matters worse, their outboard motor wouldn't start. The gale force winds quickly blew them toward the rocky shore. At the last second, Rodger jumped out and wedged himself between the rocks and water craft. Rodney, Rodger's friend, also jumped in and helped the two small boys onto the rocks. Then a man appeared to help the two boys to his house above the rocky shoreline. As the boys sat in front of a fireplace to warm up and dry off, the men secured the boat to keep it safe from the rocky shore till the storm passed. When the weather broke, they got the motor working and headed back for the trip home.

Rodger shares, "It was Rodney who eventually convinced me to attend church, and put Jesus Christ first."

Rodger might have almost lost it before he found his Savior and made him Lord of his life. So can you. Let Jesus take control of your life. You can also be a part of God's ultimate fishing creel and thus be assured of winning out for all eternity.

For a free booklet on the subject by Hank Parker called, "More Than Winning and Losing," contact us here at God's Great Outdoors by phone, mail, or e-mail. You will also receive a copy of "The Ultimate Fishing Challenge," by Jim Grassi.

HERE'S A:
"MY BIGGEST HUNTING BLUNDER" FROM
"God's Great Outdoors"
Written By Gerald Shaffner And Edited For Radio Broadcast By Gerry Caillouet
#010

Gerald Shaffner, *PSE* Prostaff Archer and seminar speaker, is one of Illinois' top whitetail deer hunters. But everything doesn't always work out for this hunter either.

In 1994, Gerald returned home from a special hunt at Clinton Lake in central Illinois. He had been hunting with two of his best buddies. While in Clinton, one of his friends tried to get him to use a new scent product, but Gerald refused. After the hunt was over and everyone was getting ready to go home, his hunting buddy again offered the scent, saying, "Take this package of scent and try it for me, I have had nothing but super response from it." So, Gerald agreed to try it.

"A couple of days after returning home, I decided to try the scent," shares Gerald. "The wind was right to hunt this area where the scent would drift into the thicket I would be hunting. I stuck one of the scent sticks in the ground and lit it, then climbed into my treestand. It was one of those perfect evenings - a slight west wind and the rut in full swing. After waiting for the scent to drift in to the area for about a half hour, I began to rattle. The result I got from antlers rattling was immediate. I hardly got my antlers hung up when I had a buck coming in on a dead run from the north. The set-up seemed to be perfect, but as quick as the buck hit the smoky scent, he stopped and started to snort. This went on for about five minutes. I have rattled in a lot of bucks, but I had never had this happen before. After about five minutes, the deer moved on down the hollow. I waited about 15 minutes and rattled to him again. He was probably 150 yards away and started snorting, this lasted for another 15 minutes, then he was gone."

Three days later, Gerald went back and hunted that area again. About 45 minutes into the hunt he spotted a big buck come out of a weed patch 30 yards south. "I picked up my antlers and rattled," continues Gerald. "The buck went back in to the woods and snorted for about 5 minutes. Was it the same buck? I don't know for sure, but a year later I hunted the area and spotted a big buck following a doe. I picked up my antlers and rattled, the response I got was the same as the previous year. I can't say it was the same deer, but if it is, I will probably never be able to rattle him in."

Gerald may have blown it on that hunt, but one hunting trip he didn't mess up on was the hunt for eternal life through Jesus Christ. You too can find success in the ultimate of hunts, the one for eternal salvation. If you would like to know more about how to find eternal life, contact us here at God's Great Outdoors by mail, phone, or e-mail and we will send you a free booklet by Charlie Alsheimer called "The Ultimate Hunt." You'll also be mailed "The Greatest Hunt of All," by Dwight Schuh.

"No Man's Land"
#010

If Satan can't win with the destruction of the Jewish people, perhaps his front line attack against Christians will be successful. The truth is, he is fighting a desperate battle and will therefore launch advances anywhere he may prove God's word, the bible, to be untrue. If Christians are stopped, the witness of the Gospel halts and so there will be no preaching of the Good News to every nation or people group as the scripture states.

Demon activity against Christians throughout the ages has been cold-blooded to say the least. Most of the very men who walked with Jesus were martyred for the cause of Christ. Church tradition teaches Peter was crucified head down as were others executed by some manner of crucifixion as well. Some Believers have been beheaded, some stoned to death. One disciple was flayed alive and another was placed in a large leather bag and dragged by ropes from behind a horse until beat to a bloody pulp. Later, killing Christians became a sport as they were executed. They all died because their lives had been transformed by the power of The Living Word they had heard, accepted and proclaimed to be true.

The devil and his demon army will be cast into the Lake of Fire where they will be tormented day and night forever and ever. They will get their just reward, but sadly the eternal punishment which was created for the fallen angels will see many unsaved men and women enter in also. They don't have to go, as the blood of Jesus Christ was shed to cover their sins, if they will only receive this free gift. As I have heard it said and it is quite true, anyone who is cast into the eternal fires of damnation are trespassing in a place created only for Satan and his demons, and have chosen to refuse the gift of God's one and only Son.

Romans 10:14,15
How, then, can they call on the one they have not believed in? And how can they believe in the one of whom they have not heard? And how can they hear without someone preaching to them? And how can they preach unless they are sent? As it is written, "How beautiful are the feet of those who bring good news!"

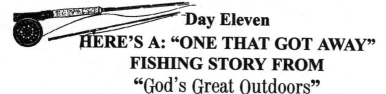

Day Eleven
HERE'S A: "ONE THAT GOT AWAY"
FISHING STORY FROM
"God's Great Outdoors"
#011

Tom Feliciano an Alaskan bush pilot and fishing guide shares two of his misadventures. The first took place on a cold and windy September day. Tom had landed his plane in the *Anti-Ak-Chak National Monument*. The *Anti-Ak-Chak* is an extinct volcano which last erupted over a hundred years ago. The volcanic cinder makes an excellent landing strip. Well, it was one of those magic days when the fishing was in Tom's own words, "Just fantastic!" The arctic char were fighting each other to get at the pink Pixie Spoon Tom's spinning gear was delivering to them with each cast.

Laying his pole on the side of the bank, Tom placed another fish on the stringer. The pole's tip hung out over the cut bank and with almost eight feet of line out, the lure hung suspended a few inches above the Alaskan peninsula's water way. Suddenly, an eight pound arctic char leapt out of the water and took off with the lure in it's mouth. Tom just managed to dive to the bank's edge in time to save his gear from going into the drink.

Another time in the shadows of the Alaskan range's *Sleeping Lady Mountains*, Tom and his son Chris, accompanied by Tom's mother, were fishing for King Salmon. On a bright and sunny spring day, Tom used his spinning gear to present gobs of fish eggs to the Kings. With a forty-five pound King on the line, Tom was playing the fish with care. After a half hour the King had worked Tom down the river. The two were heading for a bridge that crossed the Lewis River. Knowing that if the fish went under the bridge he would lose it, Tom forced it to shore. Giving the pole to his young son, he raced to the fish. Chris, not knowing how to play the beached salmon, allowed it to unhook itself and flop back in the water just as Tom arrived to watch it swim away.

Now Tom may have experienced some misadventures there, but one thing that didn't go wrong was when it came to his eternal existence after death. You too can make the right move, the move to everlasting life with our Savior and Lord Jesus Christ. You also can be a part of God's ultimate fishing creel and thus be assured of winning out for all eternity.

Let us know here at God's Great Outdoors by phone, mail, or e-mail, if you would like a free booklet on the subject by Hank Parker, called "More Than Winning and Losing." You'll also receive a free copy of "The Ultimate Fishing Challenge," by Jim Grassi.

" Crafty ideas, God gives these things to you!"

Ron Lindner

HERE'S A:
"MY BIGGEST HUNTING BLUNDER" FROM
"God's Great Outdoors"
Written By Charlie Alsheimer And Edited For Radio Broadcast
By Gerry Caillouet
#011

Charlie Alsheimer, the nationally known wildlife photographer and Field Editor for the magazine, *Deer and Deer Hunting,* remembers when he didn't practice what he preached.

"November 6th dawned perfect for hunting New York's whitetail rut - windless, 30 degrees and overcast," begins Charlie. "As I climbed into my treestand and situated myself, the last remnants of darkness began to fade. Motionless, I stood on the stand's platform waiting for shooting light to arrive. My mind wandered as I reflected on the Fall's hunt.

"........Actually, it had been brief compared to others. My bowhunting began in September when I harvested an eight point buck in Wisconsin. Was it an omen of good things to come? Unfortunately, it was not to be. On Sunday morning, October 1st, in my haste to get to the phone while dressing for church, I slipped and fell breaking my right arm. Something like this is bad enough for any avid bowhunter, but for someone who makes his living in the out-of-doors, it was tragic.

"Throughout October, I photographed and scouted hard. By the end of the month, I was able to pull my bow three times before the pain and fatigue of the injury forced me to stop shooting. Even so, my accuracy had not fallen off. On November 1st my "second" 1995 bow season began, fifteen minutes after legal shooting light I was brought back to reality by the sound of rustling leaves a distance from me. Quietly I picked my bow off of the hanger and turned to face the approaching sound. In an instant a big ten point jumped a dead fall and walked at a fast gait toward my stand. At the speed he was traveling, I knew if I didn't act fast, he'd pass my stand. Impatience did me in. Rather than wait for him to pass under my stand I decided to move as he approached. At half draw the big ten point picked up my faint movement, wheeled on his hind legs, and bounded into the brush where he stopped. Only thirty yards from me, with no shot. After a few brief moments he walked off and out of sight.

"As I sat contemplating my blunder, I couldn't help but think that I had really blown it. I knew better than to move as a buck approached. Over the years as a seminar speaker, I've told hunters time after time to wait until an approaching buck has passed before drawing the bow. Unfortunately, this 1995 blunder is a

43

classic case of 'Haste makes waste.'" Charlie may have moved too quickly on that hunt, but one hunt he did not make a mistake on was the hunt for eternal life through Jesus Christ. You can also find success in the ultimate of hunts, the one for eternal salvation. To receive a free booklet by Charlie Alsheimer called "The Ultimate Hunt," contact God's Great Outdoors by mail, phone, or e-mail. With it you'll also be sent "The Greatest Hunt of All," by Dwight Schuh.

"Temple of Doom"
#011

In the first of a series of movies about the adventurous archaeologist named Indiana Jones, the hero goes off to search for a treasure of biblical proportion, The Ark of the Covenant. His journey is commissioned when two men from Army Intelligence come to him for information only, then see he is a man who knows what is needed for the time at hand. Indy's discussion with these government officials includes the viewing of an artists rendition of a moment in the Hebrew Nation's early history. It is obvious from Jones' remarks he is no solid believer of the Bible, but only a hunter of historical artifacts, treasures for museum cases and shelves, not to fill the heart or change lives. So, if the Bible guides him to that end it has it's value.

The truth is, through the years a number of those involved in the field of archaeology considered the historical aspects of the Bible to be very inaccurate. To be more specific, they not only call into question locations and times depicted in it's pages, some of these well-educated men even doubted the existence of some of those who's names grace the pages of God's written word. For example, both King David and even Moses were believed to be only myth.

However, time and again archaeological finds have only proved the word of God as being accurate to the last detail and never has the opposite been found to be true. Today there are still those in this field of science who dispute the Bible's recorded history and so put the entire book on the shelf with other fables. They look for antiquities of dead men when sadly their hearts are dead to the truth of God and His love.

I Corinthians 3:18-20
"Do not deceive yourselves. If any one of you thinks he is wise by the standards of this age, he should become a 'fool' so that he may become wise. For the wisdom of this world is foolishness in God's sight. As it is written: 'He catches the wise in their craftiness'; and again, 'The Lord knows that the thoughts of the wise are futile.'"

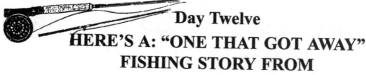

Day Twelve
HERE'S A: "ONE THAT GOT AWAY"
FISHING STORY FROM
"God's Great Outdoors"
#012

Before tournament fishing became his bread and butter, Hank Parker was still hung-up on fishing, as you'll understand. A young man of seventeen, he remembers a fishing trip to Lake Wylie, on the border of the Carolinas not far from Charlotte. On this overcast day in February the fishing was very slow. Hank was working crankbaits in the mouth of Pole Branch Creek. The flats of this bay were littered with tree stumps and one stump in particular had been in young Hank's mind as he's motored to the area. It always held bass.

Positioning the boat Hank cast to the stump and right off he has a fish on. The fish tangled in a limb that was sticking out of the water next to the stump. Believing the fish to be small, he paid the fish no mind and began pulling the limbs dead weight in. When the whole mess was at the boat's side, Hank was shocked to see the size of the fish. It was huge, and Hank adds, "The crankbait looked like a crappie jig in the bass's mouth. The bass was probably about to die of old age and this was his last meal."

Now, Hank, in looking back thinks that perhaps in his seventeen year old excitement the bass looked bigger than it really was. But in any case, he'd jerked so hard to work the limb toward the boat, all the hooks on the crankbait had pulled free but one barb and in his surprise at the fish's size, Hank relaxed the tension on the fishing line and that last hook came free letting the bass slowly swim away.

Hank Parker has been "hung-up" as a professional too. Years later, in Knoxville, TN. during the 1980's Hank was in contention to win the World's Fair Fishing Tournament. Needing only one more fish to take first place, Hank headed to an out of the way bay where he missed hooking a 8 to 9 pound bass during the pre-fishing. With one cast to where the fish hung out, Hank had him hooked. Trouble was, the bass became tangled in an old trot line that had washed into the bay from the river. Hank carefully worked the fish and all to the water craft's side and even had his hand on him when because of the tangle the bass slipped away. So too did the $50,000 first prize! Hank took home forth place and $5,000. Now Hank may not have won the Big One there, but one place he did come up a winner, and that's with the eternal salvation that comes only through Jesus Christ. For a free booklet on the subject by Hank Parker called, "More Than Winning and Losing," contact us by mail, phone, or e-mail here at God's Great Outdoors. You'll also get a copy of "The Ultimate Fishing Challenge," by Jim Grassi.

HERE'S A:
"MY BIGGEST HUNTING BLUNDER" FROM
"God's Great Outdoors"
#012

An internationally known artist whose work includes painting, sculptures, and jewelry, Max Greiner, Jr., focused his early career's efforts on wildlife art. Perhaps that had partly to do with the fact that Max was consumed with a passion for bowhunting. Having been a major player in the path modern archery has taken, which is one of the fastest growing outdoors activities today, Max's list of hunting partners appears as if a list from the "Who's Who of the Archery Hall of Fame." However, with all that "rubbing shoulders" with those famous woodsmen, it's not as if some magic has occurred. Max still makes shots that miss their intended target. Or, the wind suddenly changed directions causing the animal he is pursuing to "make like a tree and leave," when they whiff his human scent? Other times, what appears to be about to happen, is not what is about to take place, at all. Such is the case, as Max hunted for rutting bull Elk in the Routt National Forest, in an area north of Meeker, Colorado. Having backpacked in around the Pagoda Peak before the first snows of the year, this artist was daily enjoying the September beauty of God's creation. The yellowing of the quaking aspen foliage all around him, was announcing the soon to be coming "Old Man Winter."

Now Max is of the mind, bowhunters have a lot of sad stories about all the big animals that could have easily been downed had the hunter been afield with a firearm. This was the case on that backpack adventure. As his day began, he still-hunted along a side of a ridge. Suddenly about 20 yards away a very large bull, at least a six by six, appeared heading his way. What a perfect shot this was going to be, and realizing he was such a "smart bowhunter" he decided to wait and use a "trick of the trade" to harvest this magnificent bull. Max decided to wait until the elk's eyes were behind a large tree he had mentally picked out on the projected course the monarch was traveling. Max reflects on his blunder, "What I didn't know at the time was that he was going to take a hard right, straight behind the tree! I was at full draw waiting, but all I could see was giant antlers on each side of the Spruce tree's trunk, as he headed up the ridge. I was stuck behind a log jam and couldn't go anywhere." The elk had turned a 90 degree behind the tree, so all Max could do was stand and watch those very wide and heavy antlers grow smaller and smaller as the bull got further away.

Max Greiner, Jr., may have calculated incorrectly then, but in the area of locking in his position with the God who judges all men, Max is located properly. That is evident as his art work now doesn't just reflect God's creation, but also the Creator Himself, Jesus Christ who will judge the living and the dead. Are you dead in your sins? You may be seeing life's timing just like Max viewed that elk, expecting it to go one way, then turning another direction altogether. One day your next tomorrow may take a hard right, then you are no more! To learn how to cross over from life to death, contact us here at God's Great Outdoors by writing, phone, or e-mail, and we'll send a free booklet to help you by Charlie Alsheimer called, "The Ultimate Hunt." We will also send along "The Greatest Hunt of All," by Dwight Schuh.

"Against The Current"
#012

I cannot imagine a child who has spent time in Sunday School for any length of time, who has not heard the story of David and the giant he encountered. Yet, King David is still a Goliath of a stumbling block for many scholars who are skeptics of God's written word, the Bible. This is because they consider much of this book to be Israelite Mythology, until it is proven by other historical sources. So, unless the ancient Aramaean's or Philistine's writings mentioned David, he did not really exist. Before recent archaeologists discovered the earliest biblical character mentioned in secular historical records was King Ahab. But then an archaeologist discovered an ancient Aramaean inscription at the biblical city of Dan in Northern Israel dated from the ninth century B.C., bearing the name "David" and in another location a rock fragment inscribed with an ancient text made reference to the "House of David."

In fact, archaeological discoveries made in the last few years have added validity to a number of other biblical names including Moses, Jacob, Isaac, and Abraham. It would seem as more and more historical evidence is unearthed from the dust around Jerusalem and Israel, not believing in the Bible would be like swimming up stream at flood stage. One would hope with all this truth splashing these skeptics in the face, they would eventually swallow some of it.

Matthew 18:3
"And he said: 'I tell you the truth, unless you change and become like little children, you will never enter the kingdom of heaven.'"

Day Thirteen

HERE'S A: "ONE THAT GOT AWAY"
FISHING STORY FROM
"God's Great Outdoors"

Adapted From Jim Grassi's Book, *PROMISING WATERS* And Edited For
Radio Broadcast By Gerry Caillouet
#013

The founder of *Let's Go Fishing Ministries*, Jim Grassi, remembers one cold December morning in the San Francisco Bay area. Despite a weather forecast for showers and heavy fog, Jim woke early and set out to pick-up his fishing buddy, Rick. The two would be fishing the Sacramento River. When they arrived, the marina parking lot was empty, which should have been a warning to Jim about the weather conditions.

After launching the bass boat and climbing aboard, they motored off into the heavy mist. Idling along since they could not see beyond the front of their boat, they used the dark shadows of old sunken barges off the starboard side as a reference point. Following the line of submerged vessels should have led them to Jim Grassi's favorite slough. Once there, five pound Black Bass and perhaps their Striper cousins awaited them.

The biting cold and never ending fog seemed to get worse as they crossed the slough. Jim had to guess on the boat's steering with no more barges as guideposts. After five minutes, Rick broke the silence and asked Jim when they would get there. Jim tried to reassure Rick, but knew they were in trouble. They had missed the mark. After ten minutes of nothing but fog, they were both in trouble. The river current would eventually have them drifting under the Golden Gate Bridge and out to sea without anyone's notice.

Blind and in the shipping lane of very large ocean vessels, the two men soon had a close call with one of these huge freighters. Suddenly, Jim remembered his compass and map in the boat's glove box. Though lost in the fog, Jim could hear a fog horn in one direction and a train on shore in another. With those two bearings he turned the boat one hundred and eighty degrees and headed they hoped, for the marina. Moving in total faith, the two men could make out the marina's outline.

Jim Grassi, may have been lost on that fishing adventure, but there's one place he didn't get misdirected. That's with his eternal life with our Lord and Savior Jesus Christ. You also can be a part of God's ultimate fishing creel and thus be assured of winning out for all eternity. If you would like a free booklet on this subject by Hank Parker called, "More Than Winning and Losing," contact us here at God's Great Outdoors by phone, mail, or e-mail and we will be glad to see that you get one. We will also include "The Ultimate Fishing Challenge," by Jim Grassi.

HERE'S A:
"MY BIGGEST HUNTING BLUNDER" FROM
"God's Great Outdoors"
Written By Larry W. Jones And Edited For Radio Broadcast
By Gerry Caillouet
#013

Larry W. Jones, not to be confused with Larry D. Jones, is quite an elk hunter. In fact, Larry W. has also even had an elk hunt *him* out. Each winter, over a four year period, an incredibly large-racked bull drifted in out of the snow covered wilds and adopted Larry. All this time spent together is captured on two videos that he produced .... called *Rocky Mountain King* and *Elk Whisperer.* His videos are shown every place Larry speaks. But not every elk out there wants Larry around as his blunder reveals.

There they were, the hunter and the beast, face-tot-face: eight-hundred pounds of the maddest bull elk he'd ever laid eyes on. His ears were pinned back and the black hair on his back was standing straight up. His antlers loomed lethal like a dozen glistening swords ready to cut down any foe. His eyes were filled with fire and his nostrils were wet with fury. Only seven steps separated them. Seven steps and a stump; a stump that Larry W. Jones will never forget.

Larry begins... "It all started a half-hour earlier. The bull had answered my challenge from a thousand yards away. After a few bugle and grunt exchanges, it became apparent that the bull was just sounding the area. Knowing that I had to fire him up, I grabbed a pine limb and commenced to wail on the brush and trees around me. That excited him, but he wouldn't advance. He only stood his ground. The wind was in my favor so I decided to charge in as close as I could without being seen. The bull, challenged, raked and bugled himself into a rage as I drew near. I continued making challenging noises. He seemed to be at his boiling-point when I reached a small clearing in the pines about a hundred yards below his position on the brushy slope. He was making lots of crashing and thrashing noises augmented by weird chuckles, bugles and gorilla-like grunts.

"There I stood with my little stick'n'string. I had found me a big fir tree

49

stump to stand behind. Don't ask me why. It's not like it would've provided protection or anything. A man needs all the false sense of security he can get when he's standing out in the middle of a clearing and a raging bull elk is growling and a screaming like he's coming to eat you. I decided to start mimicking the old monarch. It worked! He was coming! And he was hot! When he stepped out of the thick brush at the bottom of the draw just below me, I was only thirty-eight feet up the other side. I had drawn my bow as he plowed through the last clump. He stepped out into the open, took three steps up my side, and stopped...not sure where the opposing bull was. I was a non-factor. He was simply looking right through me.

"At the exact instant that he stopped, I had just brought my drawn bow into position to take aim. But, the unthinkable had happened! The nocks of the arrows in my bow quiver had come to rest on top of the big fir stump in front of me!

"What was I to do? I tried raising up on my tip-toes, but that wasn't enough. I had to somehow aim lower. I knew if I stepped back it would be all over; he would detect unknown movement and would be gone. It was my only chance; I had to try. I made my move, but in a flash, before I could re-aim, the bull crashed down the brushy draw and was gone!" And what is Larry's consolation in the whole affair? "Oh well, who would want to clutter up a family room wall with a Pope and Young record book bull elk, anyway?"

Now Larry W. Jones may have placed his trust in an old rotten, dead stump costing him his elk, but Larry didn't blow it when he placed his trust in the Lord Jesus Christ who can take a rotten old sinner and transform him into a new and living creation. You also can be made new and have your life transformed. For a free booklet by Charlie Alsheimer called, "The Ultimate Hunt," contact us at God's Great Outdoors. Additionally, "The Greatest Hunt of All," by Dwight Schuh will be included.

"Parting The Waters Of Doubt"
#013

There is an old Irish song that speaks of traveling two different routes, the "high road" versus the "low road" on to the same destination. However, the low road seems to be the quicker or easier road as the one who travels this way gets to the end objective first. God seldom directs us on that sort of path in life. This was true when the Israelites began their exodus out of Egypt. There were at least two possible trade routes Moses and the people could have been guided to follow. The shorter coastal route by the Mediterranean would seem the logical choice.

But, God led them on the longer more difficult course. Recent archaeological digs along that shorter route have revealed numerous Egyptian military garrisons, not that God couldn't have destroyed these outposts, but what happened at the Red Sea is in the realm of impossible.

Modern technology is confirming the Bible account with infrared satellite imaging. This new science is used in modern archaeology and has traced a large migration of people, their camp locations and journey across the Sinai Peninsula and Red Sea with a correlation to the book of Exodus that is astounding! But, this isn't the only discovery slamming Biblical skeptics. Wave after wave of new finds are eroding away at the disbelief that Israel was ever even held in Egyptian captivity. Not long ago archaeologists unearthed an Israelite-style house in the location the Bible states the nation lived in slavery. Additionally, an ancient papyrus document was discovered that recounts in eye-witness fashion, the accounts of the plagues. It appears the tide of facts just keep crashing on the shore of doubt and skepticism.

Hebrews 11:6
"And without faith it is impossible to please God, because anyone who comes to him must believe that he exists and that he rewards those who earnestly seek him."

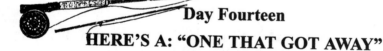

Day Fourteen
HERE'S A: "ONE THAT GOT AWAY" FISHING STORY FROM
"God's Great Outdoors"
#014

From weekend fisherman to the professional fishing circuit. Then comes your own TV show on , you guessed it, fishing. So, when you go to work you've, as the bumper sticker says, "gone fishing." Well, it might sound like some kind of dream, but for Jimmy Houston it's reality. God has opened quite a few incredible doors for this now fishing show host. But, life is still real, and in real life everything or anything can happen and often does.

Jimmy's blunder is, a laughing matter as you'll soon understand. While shooting footage for his show, he and his crew were enjoying a warm, sunny day in January. The location of this outing was Guri Lake in Venezuela. Jimmy remembers, "The temperature was between 70 and 80 degrees. Along on this trip was my good friend, Dale Wilcox. Dale was with me in my boat and the camera crew was in the other boat. Now early in the morning we had been fishing for piranha and had caught about 100 of them. Dale had joked about getting bitten as he unhooked a fish. Later, he accidentally stuck his finger in one's mouth and received a nasty bite. In the afternoon we switched to fishing for peacock bass. Landing a 21 pound fish on this lake is not uncommon. We were fishing a flooded forest area and there are a lot of tree tops sticking out of the water. Dale got hung up in one of the tree branches as we motored past. Losing his balance and knowing he was going to fall in, he jumped to one of the tree tops. Hugging the tree trunk for dear life, Dale's thoughts went back to the piranha, his bitten finger and his precarious position. Carefully, he placed first one foot, then the other into the water, hoping to find a branch on which to step on with no success. Jimmy having continued on in the boat, was laughing so hard he couldn't bring the boat around in time to save Dale from going in. So, the camera crew came to his rescue.

Jimmy Houston, may have had trouble rescuing his friend from the piranhas' jaws, but Jesus Christ had no problem saving Jimmy and countless others from the grip of an eternity in Hell. For a free booklet on the subject by Hank Parker called, "More Than Winning and Losing," contact us here at God's Great Outdoors by phone, mail, or e-mail. You will also get the "Ultimate Fishing Challenge," by Jim Grassi.

HERE'S A:
"MY BIGGEST HUNTING BLUNDER" FROM
"God's Great Outdoors"
#014

Dick Hribar (re-bar) is both a fishing guide and a fly fishing instructor. Dick also loves to go afield hunting. While his preference is the bow and arrow, this angling expert will gladly pursue big game with a firearm too! And this is where one of his mistakes occurred.

Dick and some friends were hunting big whitetail bucks in Michigan's Cranberry swamps. The seasoned woodsman was toting a new stainless steel Winchester 30-06 he'd swapped for his old hunting rifle. Dick's thoughts when he acquired the rifle were, "This is the rifle for anything I'll ever need to hunt for again, the rifle for the rest of my life."

Now, the group was hunting way back in the swamps and Dick was carrying a heavy pack filled with extra clothing as Upper Michigan gets a little cold in late November. The method for hunting was to sit and wait as the swamps are too thick to try to stalk. One evening, after many days of packing back to hunt, Dick was on his way out and was very tired. The heavy pack kept slipping and required stopping to readjust the load. Well, when he reached the truck he started unloading to put his gear in the pickup and NO RIFLE! Now Dick had carried the rifle by shoulder strap and used a walking stick to help him with the swamp's rough footing. Dick said out loud, "This is a little weird! Where's my rifle?" Thinking of all the places he'd stopped in the last several miles, he and one of his buddies turned around with two flashlights and headed back into the Cranberry swamps as the snow began to fall again. Now, when others from their group arrived, they assumed they were lost, seeing their lights in the distance, they started firing off shots to help orient them. Coming out and discussing the matter, they all agreed to call it a day, so they all went to camp. That night as Dick prayed about it, he remembered he'd come to an island in the swamp just off the main trail and readjusted his pack. He had laid the rifle against a tree. Dick could hardly wait till daylight. The next day he went in about two miles to the island and there was the rifle against the evergreen tree, all frosty from the night's cold air.

Dick Hribar may have lost his rifle for a time, but Dick will lose no time worrying about life after death as he has eternity in his grasp for keeps. You can be sure of the life hearafter too! To receive a free booklet by Charlie Alsheimer entitled, "The Ultimate Hunt," get a hold of us here at God's Great Outdoors by mail, phone, or e-mail and we'll be glad to send you a copy. We will also send a copy of "The Greatest Hunt of All," by Dwight Schuh.

"Humpty Dumpty"
#014

A children's fable tells of an egg-headed sort of fellow who sits on a wall, that is of course, until his great fall. Then, try as they might, the king's subjects cannot reassemble their fallen comrade. The Bible speaks of a great fall too. The collapse of the walls of Jericho are the first battle after the Israelites cross over into the Promised Land. Then the army of God attacks and destroys every living thing in the city in compliance with God's command.

For many years scholars denied that this event ever occurred. Archaeological text books stated the absence of the biblical Jericho as proof that the Bible was not historically correct. They believed the city was not that old. Yet, recent evidence excavated by archaeologists reveal the city did indeed exist during Joshua's day. But that isn't all they found. The walls appeared to have fallen outward from the city and down flat, which formed a sort of a ramp to usher in the Israelite army.

According to the Bible, as the troops invaded Jericho they burned the city, including all the stores of grain, as God had forbidden them from carting off any loot. And this too has been confirmed by archaeological discovery. This additional evidence indicates the city fell in a short siege, and it is very strange that the invading troops didn't carry off the stores of food, but scattered and burned them.

Some have suggested an earthquake felled the walls of Jericho, but whoever heard of walls being laid flat in such a catastrophic event? It appears more to indicate the hand of the Almighty God who loves us so much he has done such things to help collapse any doubts that His word, the Bible is true.

Romans 3:23,24
"for all have sinned and fall short of the glory of God, and are justified freely by his grace through the redemption that came by Christ Jesus."

Day Fifteen
HERE'S A: "ONE THAT GOT AWAY"
FISHING STORY FROM
"God's Great Outdoors"
#015

If you have ever bought ice fishing equipment, there is an excellent chance *H.T. Enterprises* is the company who manufactured it. Paul Grahl is the president of this busy business which works hard to make the fishing action hot when the temperatures are cold. But, Paul Grahl doesn't limit himself to just below zero angling. He'll also take to the water when the only ice to be found is in a chest full of pop. The fact is, Paul's "One That Got Away" Fishing Story is one that he's thankful got away.

He'd waited practically an entire year to take his best friend from Korea, Mr. Kang, fishing. This business acquaintance of over twelve years arrived to visit with Paul in early April, 1999. The two set out for a small semi-private lake; as Paul had a rowboat stored there. The water teamed with bass and some great perch. A very nice lake to fish on, but the men also looked forward to the peaceful time that lay ahead, or so they thought.

With anticipation of what was to come, they flipped the boat over. Suddenly, Mr. Kang got excited and cried out, "Paul! Snake! Snake!" knowing full well that

Paul doesn't like snakes. The thirty plus inch Garter snake set the two to work with oars, trying to fish him out of the boat. Paul reflects, "I don't want to sound cruel, but he was in the wrong place at the wrong time. He ended up lifeless after two people did a very frantic job of trying to get him out." Thinking all was well, they loaded the gear and shoved off on that bright, beautiful evening. Moving out to twenty feet of water, Paul was enjoying the time. He was rowing, looking a different direction from the back of the boat, when he heard Mr. Kang in the stern let out a scream. A three foot Garter snake - snaked out of the back of the transom, moving toward Mr. Kang. Paul states, "Maybe if I lived in the bayous of Louisiana that might not be quite so alarming, but in Wisconsin this is a once in a lifetime experience." Both men sprung up for positions of safety onto the middle boat seat as the boat now rested in the middle of the lake. There, two frightened, older men almost tipping the boat over, frantically grabbed oars to remove this menace. Paul adds, "I'm sorry ladies, you'd think it was a mouse." The pair began doing a dance as the serpent kept coming at them. Close to tipping several times, the fight lasted five minutes. Paul concludes, "If anyone on shore would have seen us they would have reported us to an institution! Finally, we flung it into the lake. If anyone would have asked us what we were doing we would have said, 'One time a year we come out and do a cultural dance.' We laughed so hard later."

The fishing ended right then for fear of another snake coming out of hiding and Paul now has his boat stored to prevent future incidents. But Paul Grahl's biggest victory over a serpent, was over Satan, when he surrendered his life to Jesus Christ. You too can do the same. To receive a free booklet on the subject contact us here at God's Great Outdoors by mail, phone, or e-mail and we will send you "More Than Winning & Losing," by Hank Parker as well as "The Ultimate Fishing Challenge," by Jim Grassi.

HERE'S A:
"MY BIGGEST HUNTING BLUNDER" FROM
"God's Great Outdoors"
#015

John West is now retired from the business, but John's wife, Sheila is President of *Archery Center International* an archery product distributor which ships to buyers in all fifty states and many foreign countries too. So, in the autumn, if John is getting a little in the way, Sheila insists John take his bow and go hunting somewhere! Well as you can imagine, John doesn't have to be told twice.

One of those "somewheres" was on a elk hunt in the middle of September, with the late summer temperature in the 60 degree range. John had joined his good friend Larry D. Jones of *Wilderness Sound Productions*, in Arizona. The two were hunting hard the way they both like it and the bulls were big and fired up!

Spotting some cows, the pair called with diaphragm calls, grunting and bugling as they moved in on the herd. Larry told John, "This is going to be your chance, I can just listen to him and tell!" John's reply was, "Ok, fine!" Larry likes to get right into the middle of things. Cows were ten to fifteen feet away as they tried to get the bull to come closer. John says, "That's the way Larry likes to hunt, he likes it exciting and I do too." With Larry 30 feet away calling, he had the herd bull "riled up!" The bull approached and he was a dandy, 320 Pope & Young points, with beautiful white-tipped antlers which were easy to judge as he stopped 18 yards from John.

Before arriving in Arizona, John had practiced diligently everyday and his shooting was just automatic. The three pins on his bow sight were dead-on. Now as he let the arrow fly, it went right over the elk's back. The bull and cows scattered, sounding like a stampede, and John hung his head. He had the sight pin centered in the bull's chest, what had happened? Had his arrow been sent off course by an unseen branch?

After that, Larry and John had gone off hunting in different directions. Around one in the afternoon, John, with the breeze in his face, started to smell elk. On calling, John brought in another 6X6 bull to 18 yards, who just happened to stick his head in a bush and began feeding. "Picture perfect." "Man, how good does it get!?," John said to himself. Pulling to full-draw and putting the pin on the target, he released and watched the arrow again sail over the bull's back, "As pretty as you please!" remembers John. This time he was sure there were no limbs to deflect his arrow, he was ready to cry. He sat down and thought about it. Then stood up and reenacted the shot, putting the red pin in the center of the now, memory only, elk. Then it hit him, the red pin was for forty yards and the white pin was for twenty yards. "You dummy!" he thought. Hiking back to the truck he changed the red pin with the white because he discovered his eye picked up red better in the sunlight. John said, "Red is dead." and the next day John downed a beautiful 5X6.

Now in John West's case, when it comes to his sight pin, red may be dead, but for his eternal life it's reversed. Red is life when John, or you too, for that matter come under the blood of Jesus Christ. The blood that was poured out for our sins, can save you just as it has saved John West. To receive a free booklet by Charlie Alsheimer called, "The Ultimate Hunt," that will explain how you too can find eternal life through Jesus Christs' shed blood, contact us here at

God's Great Outdoors by mail, phone, or e-mail. You will also receive "The Greatest Hunt of All," by Dwight Schuh.

"Fact Is...."
#015

Many of the things we were taught and our children are still taught today, are presented as fact. The truth is however, much of the time the fact is only a theory, as scientists are at the end of the knowledge they have on that subject at that given time. The root of the problem is not what we know, but in what it is we assume we know.

In the early 1900's a chemical test for Benzene was a simple color-change reaction which when given supposedly meant that Benzene was present. Well, one day a graduate student subjected Benzene to a series of distillations. With each distillation he obtained a slightly purer sample. After numerous purifications he subjected his almost pure Benzene sample to the standard color test. But, there was no color change which would indicate a negative test for Benzene.

His professor believed the student was in error as the test had to work. The distillation was repeated with another graduate student as observer. With each step documented, the end product again failed to give a positive color change for Benzene. It turned out the impurities and not the Benzene gave the color change. Yet, books published over fifty years later still gave this test as a way to check for the presence of Benzene.

Remember, once the atom was the smallest particle in existence, then sub-atomic particles were discovered. Is that the end, with sub-atomic particles being the smallest? And what holds atoms together anyway? What made an electron negatively charged and a proton positively charged and what put these two opposite forces together? What prevents these minute particles from flying apart? The point is, don't put so much store in science, as we know so little and what little we do know is subject to change. Instead, put your trust in God.

Colossians 1:16,17
"For by him all things were created: things in heaven and on earth, visible and invisible, whether thrones or powers or rulers or authorities; all things were created by him and for him. He is before all things, and in him all things hold together."

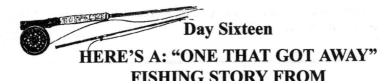

Day Sixteen

HERE'S A: "ONE THAT GOT AWAY" FISHING STORY FROM "God's Great Outdoors"

#017

Ex-*Cincinnati Reds* catcher, Brian Dorsett, remembers the time his boat almost got away. It happened quite a few years ago, while Brian was in college. He and a neighbor friend took off on one of their usual fishing trips. Mike Watson and Brian loaded an old John boat in the back of the pick-up and down the road they went.

Brian states, "It was a beautiful, sunny day in late spring. Perfect weather for fishing." Leaving their home in Terre Haute, Indiana they whizzed down the highway. But their trip was about to be interrupted. Had the two young men failed to tie the boat down properly or what, Brian doesn't know, but looking in his rearview mirror, Brian Dorsett could see the John boat had gone airborne about twenty feet above the road way. The water craft landed on the pavement and with sparks flying came to a stop in the path of the vehicle behind them. The driver of an old pick-up slammed on his brakes and skidded to a stop. However, an old engine in the pick-up's bed proceeded to advance forward, right into the rear of the old pick-up's cab. Praise God no one was hurt. Just hot under the collar.

After apologizing to the other driver, the two men reloaded the scratched, but otherwise seaworthy craft back into their pick-up truck. After arriving at the favorite farm pond they both had a great day fishing, catching several nice large mouth bass.

Now Brian Dorsett may have almost lost it when it came to his John boat, and he's lost a baseball game or two. But one place he didn't lose it, and that's where it comes to his eternity through Jesus Christ. You can also be assured of an eternal home and thus have the peace that passes all understanding. For a free booklet on the subject by Hank Parker, titled "More Then Winning and Losing," contact us here at God's Great Outdoors by phone, mail, or e-mail and you will also be sent "The Ultimate Fishing Challenge," by Jim Grassi.

HERE'S A:
"MY BIGGEST HUNTING BLUNDER" FROM
"God's Great Outdoors"
#016

High in the Colorado mountains, Ken Beck, the owner of the *Black Widow Bow Company*, remembers a hunt that left him suffering from the effects of exposure. With the September weather edging in the Fall season, the quaking aspens were just starting to turn their Autumn yellow. The primary objective on this wilderness adventure was a chance at bringing down a bull elk. But in the evenings, Ken would slip down to the edge of an alfalfa field to try his hand at the mule deer that came there to feed.

Arising very early every morning, hiking up and down the ridges and dining for over a week on camp food, Ken says, "I was not eating well. At noon I was digging through the picked over pantry cooler. I found a container of grape juice concentrate everyone else had overlooked, so I mixed it up. Well, it tasted mighty good, too good I'm afraid because I probably over did it and drank too much."

That evening on the walk to the alfalfa field, Ken suddenly started to experience a distressful feeling in his lower digestive tract. Feeling like two huge bull elk fighting for control of a harem of cows, the intestinal activity brought an abrupt halt to Ken's advance. Ken felt one of the bull's had lost the fight and was on a hard run to escape. Quickly placing his bow and hunting gear down, Ken heeded nature's call out in the middle of the open sage brush flat.

In this awkward situation, hunkered down among the low sage bushes, Ken spied "a nice little 4x4 muley buck" feeding his way. Why not try for a shot he thought, so slowly Ken reached for his bow and nocked an arrow. By this time, the buck was feeding behind some taller sage 20 yards away. His only shot required rising to a standing position. Being self-conscious of his exposure, which in turn effected his concentration, Ken continues, "Flustered I shot at least a foot over the buck's back. I had to chuckle at the whole thing and how silly I must have looked. But the buck never did see me, even as white as my lily white skin was."

Ken may have missed the mark on that hunt, but one hunting trip he didn't miss out on was the hunt for eternal life through Jesus Christ. You also can find success in the ultimate of hunts, the one for eternal salvation. For a free booklet by Charles Alsheimer, contact us here at God's Great Outdoors by mail, phone, or e-mail. We 'll send "The Greatest Hunt of All," by Dwight Schuh too!

"It Doesn't Add Up"
#016

When I was in college I was majoring in Biology with the dream of one day becoming a Wildlife Biologist. I hoped to work for a Fish and Wildlife Department somewhere with lots of opportunities to fish and hunt game I would never have the chance to pursue in my home state of Maryland. Before I transferred to the University of Maryland, I attended Prince George's Community College to bag as many of the requirements I would need in my future's quest. It was in the Biology 101 class that a major turning point in my belief system started to take what would become a 180 degree turn. We were learning about how the way life just suddenly happened billions of years ago, you know, the ammonia based atmosphere, lightning, and seawater. Put the three together and you get amino acid or so we were told. After all, no one had to sell Evolution to me, as I came to college already a believer of this scientific truth, I was not a believer in God.

When we arrived at Natural Selection, for the first time a red flag went up in my mind. My professor explained that 99.99% of all mutations were detrimental to the species. In other words, when an offspring is born with physical change from the parents, it is going to die! That meant that only .01% will live. Our teacher was able to give several examples of defects that caused the newborn to perish. But only one of a mutation that was a benefit. But was it?

The professor related a story of a farmer in England who had a lamb born with very short legs. So, he bred a variety of short-legged sheep so farmers wouldn't need fences that were as high. "Wait a minute!," I thought. I was a hunter and right away pictured big horn sheep in my mind. A short-legged lamb would be the first one a cougar would catch when an attack on the flock occurred. In the wild this wasn't a benefit, so the mathematical percentage to me seemed to point against Evolution. The seeds of doubt were planted and began to grow.

Romans 1:25
"They exchanged the truth of God for a lie, and worshiped and served created things rather than the Creator—who is forever praised. Amen."

Psalm 145:18
"The Lord is near to all who call on him, To all who call to him in Truth."

Day Seventeen
HERE'S A: "ONE THAT GOT AWAY" FISHING STORY FROM
"God's Great Outdoors"

Written By Steve Chapman And Edited For Radio Broadcast By Gerry Caillouet
#018

Steve Chapman's experience happened when he was about fifteen years old. He was invited by a West Virginia gentleman to fish for catfish. Because of the distance from his home, Steve would have to stay the night. Besides the fishing, there was a daughter his own age. Steve begins, "Her long blonde hair flowed like a mountain brook, her eyes were more lovely than speckled trout and her voice was sweeter than the sound of a bass dancing on top of the water - I was hooked." The room Steve was given was in the middle of the house, an area folks had to pass through on their way to breakfast. So, when the wake-up call came, Steve's modest nature dictated that he dress under the covers. He tried to hurry before "she" came by.

With his duffle bag at the bed's side, Steve quickly went to work. Steve continues, "I dug through and got my pants and wrestled them on to my bare legs. The next step would be to get my sweater out and slip it over my T-shirt. I reached into the bag, felt for the sweater, started to pull it out and was puzzled at the resistance I encountered in trying to remove it. I yanked a couple of times and something held the sweater in the bag. I got a new grip on it and gave it one more pull. **THEN IT HAPPENED!** An artificial lure I brought from home had fallen out of it's container. It was a large lure with treble hooks on front and rear. The rear set of hooks was attached to the bag and the front set to the sweater. A hook on the front set buried into my thumb up to my elbow (Well, that's what it felt like!). There was only one way to respond to the disaster, **SCREAM!** Of course the world came running to my bed of affliction and there I lay, caught like a carp. "SHE," was standing there with the crowd and modest me was only half dressed. In the midst of my pain, I could see that for some reason everyone, including "her," had two emotions on their faces. First, there was sympathy, which I desperately needed, secondly however, out there in the far corners of their mouths, there seemed to be the slight traces of the effect that humor has on humans. That smirk that precedes all out laughter was making their faces twitch like Elvis."

After being rescued and taken to a nearby clinic, Steve had to endure both medical treatment and jokes. The worst one, "Steve, I hear the girl you like loves to fish and she's really into the catch and release method!"

Steve Chapman made a big mistake then, but when he set his anchor on eternal life with Jesus Christ, he was hooked for keeps! For a free booklet on the subject by Hank Parker called, "More Than Winning and Losing," contact us here at God's Great Outdoors by phone, mail, or e-mail and we'll also send you a booklet by Jim Grassi called, "The Ultimate Fishing Challenge."

HERE'S A:
"MY BIGGEST HUNTING BLUNDER" FROM
"God's Great Outdoors"
#017

As a free-lance cameraman who has done shooting for *Realtree Productions,* Dave Hoferts' hunting seasons are quite full with traveling to locations and working with projects on his own digital video camera and editing system. While a student at Ohio's *Cedarville College*, David Hofert was also wearing several other hats. Dave had a major part in production of God's Great Outdoors radio program while at *Cedarville*. When not studying for college exams or editing interviews of Gerry Caillouet and his guests, David put on a camouflaged cap and ventured into the nearby wood lots.

In the autumn of Dave's sophomore year, he and four other students he hunted with were quite successful hunting the local whitetail deer population and that's where their blunder began. You see with no other place to go to process the harvest God had given them, these outdoorsmen decided to use the college campus grounds and their dorm to skin and butcher the deer. So, with the animal hanging from the soccer goal post, the wiley woodsmen skinned and quartered the deer. Then carrying the sections up to their dorm, they went to work cutting and wrapping the prize in an assembly line style operation. With the meat stored in the resident director's freezer, the successful hunters were able to dine on fried venison steaks wrapped in bacon, whenever they desired. This, Dave said, was the group's favorite way of serving the wild gourmet.

All was going well until they tried to move their operation into another dorm. Some of the students in that dorm didn't care for having their bathroom turned into a "meat processing plant." So, a call to campus security was their undoing. When the school officials were informed, all five young men received e-mail messages making it clear all such activities on college grounds must stop! The next year a paragraph was added to the resident assistant's handbook stating that "No wild game is to be butchered on the college campus." Dave says that's how he and the others left their mark at *Cedarville College*.

Well, David Hofert may not have thought through his actions then, but one place David did act correctly, that's where it comes to peace and eternal life in Jesus Christ. You too can have the peace that passes all understanding. For a free booklet on the subject by Charlie Alsheimer called, "The Ultimate Hunt," contact us here at God's Great Outdoors, by mail, phone, or E-mail. You will also be sent "The Greatest Hunt of All," by Dwight Schuh.

"The X File Factor"
#017

After my first visit to Washington State, I found myself gazing out the window of the airliner as it lifted off from the Portland, Oregon airport. Soon we were above the cloud cover and all that remained visible of this Northwestern state was the high mountain peaks which included Mount St. Helen. The eruption of this volcano blew numerous holes in the belief that the earth is billions of years old. Knowledge of this event opened up a discussion with the man seated next to me. We talked about this and also Creation vs. Evolution.

I pointed out to him the incredible aircraft we both sat in and how silly I would be considered if I told him that it just happened by chance. That at one time all the parts sat in a hanger and over many years the pieces came together as we saw them and one day the engines fired up and the old bird was ready to fly. He agreed that clearly there had been a designer and parts made in many different places were sent to a central location for assembly, and that it was no accident and man is even more complex than a jet.

In college I read many books about UFO's and the history of their sightings and so on. Funny thing was, these authors also addressed the fact that the science of archaeology had yet to find the so called "missing link" from ape to man. And these writers had the answer for that too. They said that aliens had landed on our planet and had a big shore party, if you will, with the "wildlife" on their trek through space and you and I are the result. They went on to state that this is why there has never and will never be a fossil found of a transitional life form from an ape-like animal to Homosapien. This idea struck a negative cord in me as apparently these UFO's buffs were unaware that even when similar creatures like mule deer and whitetail deer cross breed their offspring are sterile. Therefore, this reasoning, as does evolution in general, requires more faith than a belief in Creation and a loving God, who made man in His own image.

Ephesians 2:10
"For we are God's workmanship created in Christ Jesus to do good works which God prepared in advance for us to do."

63

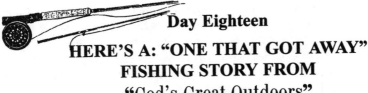

Day Eighteen

HERE'S A: "ONE THAT GOT AWAY" FISHING STORY FROM "God's Great Outdoors"
#020

Jack Arthur has caught one for the book, record book that is, as he holds a record for a large King Salmon he once caught. As a "fisher-of- men", Jack has worked with his wife Kay, of *Precept Ministries* to make an incredible impact by teaching God's Word around the world. But when Jack takes time to get away, he's usually wetting a line somewhere, and Alaska is a favorite choice.

One time while fishing on Kodiac Island with a missionary friend, Willie Hindrick and two others, their arrival seemed to be timed just right. 30-40 lb. migrating salmon were swimming around them as they fished and in no time two nice fish were lying on the gravel bank awaiting the walk back to the cabin for supper. Plans changed however, when a 600 lb. brown bear sow with two 100 lb. cubs appeared on the opposite bank. The sow was no stranger to fishermen and began beating on the grass as if begging for the fish they'd landed. When the sow and cubs began to cross the river, Jack was already moving quickly upstream and was almost 100 yards away. But, his good friend Willie had not moved away from the threatening situation as fast. Jack yelled to his old friend, "Willie come on, she's going to catch up to ya!" Jack remembers, "About that time Willie came flying toward me as fast as his hip boots flopping along would allow." The bear and cubs ate the two fish that were left unattended and soon came looking for what else the fishermen could provide. At this point a brave woman who had arrived with another group of fishermen chased off the cubs and sow by banging two frying pans together. But the next couple of days the returning mother bear and her youngsters ate 13 fish the men had caught.

The last day, Jack lay in the cabin sick in bed when he saw the sow's nose sticking under the entrance door. Jack grabbed two frying pans and began slamming them together right next to the bear's sniffer. It worked, but the group sent out prayers to God and kept a watchful eye out until the float plane arrive.

Jack Arthur may have lost in the area of fish to bring home, but one place he didn't go empty handed, and that is when it comes to the area of life eternal. For a free booklet by Hank Parker called, "More Than Winning and Losing," contact us here at God's Great Outdoors by mail, phone, or e-mail and we will send you one. You get "The Ultimate Fishing Challenge," by Jim Grassi too!

HERE'S A:
"MY BIGGEST HUNTING BLUNDER" FROM
"God's Great Outdoors"
#018

You would think the owner and president of the largest selling, bag-style archery target company, *Morrell Mfg. Inc.*, would always hit the bull's eye. Well, you would think so, but Dale's access to an assortment of targets manufactured by his company, no matter how much time he might put in on the archery range, does not transform him into the "Bionic Bowman," as he is still human.

But the occasional arrow missing it's mark is not his most nagging problem when it comes to pursuing trophy class whitetail bucks. Dale has to continue to remind himself to not move or look around too much and to always stay alert while deer hunting. Time and again, he has blown it on big bucks, spikes, and does too, all because of not being alert constantly. It has plagued him so many times, it's hard to pick just one incident, but there was one, and he didn't have to travel far as it happened in his home state of Arkansas.

Dale was hunting during the middle of November on a partly cloudy day. The leaves had about completed their transformation to the assorted God-given colors, and for the most part had let go and sailed to the ground leaving the trees quite bare. This factor could have added to Dale's problem, which he has named "The relaxed mode." Dale states, "I can only sit in the stand for two or three hours, at the most. I've done the 'all day' sitting before, I can't do that." Well, Dale's treestand was hanging 15 ft. above the forest floor as several does came working their way through the location he was hunting. As the does moved off, even though the rut was in, Dale let his guard down and shifted his body position. That is when a very respectable 10 point buck that was there all along caught Dale's movement and snorted him back to full alert. But, it was too late. The buck stomped his hoof and departed for places unknown.

Dale may have moved at the wrong time then, but his timing wasn't off when it comes to asking Christ Jesus to save him from an eternity of separation from God, in Hell. You also can have that same assurance and the timing is right for you too! For a free booklet on the subject by Charlie Alsheimer called, "The Ultimate Hunt," write, call, or E-mail us here at God's Great Outdoors. We will also include "The Greatest Hunt of All," written by Dwight Schuh.

"Cuckoo-Cuckoo-Cuckoo"
#018

One of my hardest struggles in college was in mathematics. Don't ask me why, but doing some of the math associated with the science classes I was taking, almost killed me. My head literally would hurt from the problems, especially Analytical Chemistry. Be that as it may, despite my difficulty with the number side of science, I understood just how important it was to verify facts in any area of scientific research.

I was being taught, mathematically speaking, that only a tiny fraction of the mutations that occur resulted in an advancement of anyone given species. It seemed to me kind of like playing Russian Roulette with a pistol only lacking one bullet. The possibility would be difficult enough for just one animal species, but there wasn't only one species. With over 15,000 known species of protozoa, 625,000 different kinds of insects, 5,000 species of reptiles, 30,000 birds, 40,000 different fish species, and 12,000 species of mammals; the probability of all these creatures reaching their given level of evolution would have to decrease, I would think. And don't forget all the species of plant life found around the world.

I learned later that the chance of just one species evolving is equal to taking a wind-up alarm clock apart and placing it into your clothes dryer, then running that appliance until the timepiece has reassembled, is wound-up, running, and set at the correct time. It's not impossible mathematically speaking, you'll just need a whole lot of time and a good measure of faith as you stand and wait for it to happen!

Romans 1:20
"For since the creation of the world God's invisible qualities – his eternal power and divine nature – have been clearly seen, being understood from what has been made so that men are without excuse."

Hebrews 4:13
"Nothing in all creation is hidden from God's sight. Everything is uncovered and laid bare before the eyes of him to whom we must give account."

Day Nineteen

HERE'S A: "ONE THAT GOT AWAY"
FISHING STORY FROM
"God's Great Outdoors"
Written By Bill D. Blackmon And Edited For Radio Broadcast
By Gerry Caillouet
#021

Bill Blackmon and his wife, Jennie, own and operate *Katche* (catch-ee) *Camp Outfitters,* a four hour drive north of Saskatoon, Saskatchewan. Bill has a fine operation with very new and up-to-date equipment, but sometimes someone wants to use their own stuff, which may have the potential to leave Bill in a bad way. Bill's blunder begins like this, "I strongly prefer to guide my fishing clients using my own boat and equipment, but these very nice grandparents had a new boat and were eager to have their five-year old grandson catch a fish, so I agreed to be their trusty guide with their equipment.

"I knew this was going to be a different experience when I arrived at their new yacht and was greeted by a snarling Doberman Pincer, who I had not been informed of, but who was most certainly part of this happy family. (Uh-oh! Things began to click!) 'Don't worry, Bill, old 'Mako' wouldn't hurt a flea!' (Yeah, right!, thought Bill)

"The five-year old was hyper exuberant and had especially neat fishing tackle. He had a three foot rod with a genuine Mickey Mouse reel. You turned Mickey's ears to retrieve line! As any rusty prophet could predict, we soon had three happy fishermen sharing an 18 foot opening which, by the way, was the only opening in the spacious canopy of this freshwater craft which would allow one to put the line overboard. Sure enough, the young grandson snagged a four-pound Northern Pike with his Mickey Mouse big game fishing machine and Captain Blackmon's expert advice. The old pike rolled and circled, and before you could say 'Yikes!,' he had all three lines in one large continuous disaster. The Doberman up to this point had been quietly laying in the boat and periodically growling." Bill continues, "As I worked the fish into the boat, the dog went completely berserk. In the ensuing melee, young grandson, thoroughly delighted, gave a mighty heave which brought the fish along with three lines and three large lures filled with hooks upon the top of Grandpa's new canopy. The dog jumped on top of the canopy with the fish flopping and twisting. Grandpa said, 'Bill, DO SOMETHING!' Actually, several things came to mind.

"After I separated dog from fish from line from hooks from canopy, Grandson yelled, 'Man! This fishing is fun!' "

And so it was.

Now Bill Blackmon may have made the wrong choice by letting this "family" use it's own boat, but Bill didn't go in the wrong direction when it comes to his position regarding eternal life. Bill chose to anchor his life in Jesus Christ and you can too. To receive a free booklet on the subject by Hank Parker called, "More Than Winning And Losing," contact us by mail, phone, or e-mail here at God's Great Outdoors. Plus, you'll also receive "The Ultimate Fishing Challenge," by Jim Grassi.

HERE'S A:
"MY BIGGEST HUNTING BLUNDER" FROM
"God's Great Outdoors"
#019

The *Hodgdon Powder Company* traces it's beginning not back to the time the Chinese invented gun powder, but the year of 1946. Bob Hodgdons' parents started this now multi-million dollar company in their home. The mail order business' work began in the basement, and Bob and his brother would take 100 pound kegs to the rail yard every morning on their way to school. From there, they were shipped off to the customers. Today Hodgdon Powder Company sends smokeless propellents all over the world.

Another product this company manufacturers is Pyrodex. This is a replacement propellent for black powder enthusiasts, and Bob Hodgdon, who is now the president of *Hodgdon Powder Company* is one of the many muzzle loading shooters who go afield with Pyrodex backing their projectile loads.

The sport of muzzle loading is becoming more and more popular as hunting seasons are set-up just for those who limit themselves to this primitive firearm. Also, match shooting, where marksmen compete against each other to see who is the top shooter is growing. But, sometimes the best of shots on the target range can miss in the field, and that's true even when you are president of the company making the powder you ram down your smoke pole.

Bob's hunting blunder happened some time ago on a September antelope hunt in Wyoming. The group of four hunters was whittled down to half because of an automobile accident two of his friends who were to meet them experienced in route, one of them being almost killed. The men had all looked forward to spending time together and sharing the experience of the hunt as well. So, the first day out, Bob and his friend, Doug Delsemme, the company lawyer, headed out alone. The temperature was a pleasant 70 degrees in the late afternoon as the two crossed a ravine in search of their goal, a dandy pronghorn buck. As the pair came up out of the ravine, they came face-to-face with almost thirty-five antelope grazing along, the band of "lopes" paid surprisingly very little attention to the intruders. With their prey at only forty yards too, both went for their muzzle loading six shooters instead of the rifles they had been carrying along. With each picking out a buck, Bob states, "I still don't know who fired first, but we both emptied our guns and neither of us hit our animal."

To add insult to injury, when the smoke cleared, the band of pronghorns moved off slowly - didn't run - didn't care. Both men are excellent shots, and these were easy shots with the sun behind the men - who can say what happened? The two redeemed themselves later as each harvested a nice buck - with their rifles, however!

Now Bob Hodgdon may have missed the mark that day and several other times too, but one place he didn't miss was with everlasting life. He's free from the smoke that will roll up from the fires of Hell, and you can be too! To receive a free booklet on the subject called "The Ultimate Hunt," by Charlie Alsheimer, contact us here at God's Great Outdoors by mail, phone, or e-mail. You will also be sent Dwight Schuh's, "The Greatest Hunt of All".

"Cock-A-Doodle-Do!"
#019

What came first, the chicken or the egg? Seems like a child's riddle, but if one is to take evolution seriously, it is a legitimate question. Before we go there however, did you know that scientists can measure how many tons of sediment flows down the Mississippi River each year? If the earth is billions of years old as we are told (scientists can't agree, 2-20 billion years is the present range, I believe) the amount of sediment traveling down the Old Swanny would mean the continent of North America would have eroded away at least seven times! And if the Mississippi is as old as the Colorado River, why isn't there a Grand Canyon there too?

Then there is the cosmic dust that falls on the earth each year. The same amount falls on the moon too. So, the Lunar Lander was designed with pads on the legs to set on over 100 feet of dust as calculated by the billions of years scientists thought the "Man in the Moon" has been smiling down on the earth. However, the less than an inch of dust found on the moon if calculated backwards, equals what the Bible says about a very young earth, about six thousand years old.

The desert yucca plant and the pronba moth both depend on each other for their very existence. The plant for pollination and the moth for food to the hatching caterpillars. On top of this, there are several species of yucca plants and each species is dependent on it's own species of moth. There are numerous other plant-animal relationships that depend totally on each others co-existence. Who came first? No, they would have had to evolve at the same times, wouldn't they?

About the chicken and the egg question. Well, the egg and chicken is only two-thirds the only question. Which came first, the chicken, the egg or the rooster who was needed to fertilize the egg? Did the male evolve along side of the female? This makes the question much tougher unless you remember that God is the Creator who spoke the world, and everything in it, into existence.

Hebrews 1:10
"He also says, 'In the beginning, O Lord, you laid the foundations of the earth, and the heavens are the work of your hands.'"

Day Twenty
HERE'S A: "ONE THAT GOT AWAY"
FISHING STORY FROM
"God's Great Outdoors"
#022

When you watch a fishing or hunting program on television, view a video, or pick-up a magazine on the same subject, there is a chance some of what's presented will include tips on different outdoor products to help your outings be more fun and successful. This is done to enhance the story idea the producer or writer is trying to get across. So, you're not only entertained, but also educated.

Well, amidst those sportsmen shows and magazines are the commercials we've all become so accustomed to expect. After all, it's advertising dollars that make production and printing of the various forms of outdoor entertainment we enjoy possible. And it's that equipment that helps you on your own adventures. That way you'll have those exciting times to look forward to also.

Tripp Advertising located near Minnesota's Twin Cities is one of those companies whose job it is to get the product idea across to the public's mind correctly - and quickly. After all, "Time is money." Being busy in the business of doing this type of work, the president, Howard Tripp, always looks forward with anticipation to his times afield or stream. So, no matter what form of media presentation he's dabbling with, when his time to get away arrives, he's off.

Now Howard's fishing fiasco was one that almost caused him to see fireworks. Not in the sky mind you, but from his wife. And, it would be no coincidence that it happened on the fourth of July. He and his bride Julie, were fishing Wisconsin's Lake Lac Courte Oreillea (La-Coo-D-Ray). It was hot and windless, as the two were out fishing for Muskie that day. Muskellunge are the largest cousins in the pike family. How large do they get? Well, Wisconsin's state record is over sixty-nine pounds! Big enough to dine on muskrats and ducks, which they do. It was probably no new state record that followed Howard's buck tail to the side of the boat that Independence Day, but it was an eye popping, trophy fish. So much so, that Howard rushed to cast to it again. However, his reel back lashed, and instead of his lure landing in the deep, it landed deep in his mate's blonde hair, or at least that is what she thought.

Horrified, Howard could see the blood flowing from the lure's hook, which was sunk in his wife's ear. Julie exclaimed, "Get this out of my hair!" Looking at her husband's shocked face, Julie asked, "Did you stick that in me?" "Honey sit down." was his reply. Julie questioned, "Why did you stick me...." and she sat down. Howard states, "As I watched the blood run down her neck, the look on her face could have ignited a fire!" At the hospital in Hayward, Wisconsin, the doctor who attended them was so frail he could not muster the strength to cut through the big muskie-sized hooks, so Howard had to undo what he did by cutting the hooks himself. With the damage repaired, both physically and emotionally, Julie exuberantly announced, "Let's go back fishing!" and so they did. Neither one catching any muskie or each other the rest of the outing.

Now the fiery anger of his wife was a short lived experience, but the fires of Hell last an eternity. Howard has escaped them forever and you can too. To receive a free booklet on the subject by Hank Parker called, "More Than Winning and Losing," contact us here at God's Great Outdoors by mail, phone, or e-mail and we will also send "The Ultimate Fishing Challenge," by Jim Grassi.

HERE'S A:
"MY BIGGEST HUNTING BLUNDER" FROM
"God's Great Outdoors"
#020

Dick Kirby, the President and owner of *Quaker Boy Game Calls*, went from cutting hair to cutting on calls aimed at a lovesick Tom Turkey. Now, Dick is good at "turkey talk," so good he, in his early days won a number of national turkey calling contests. But as he seasoned in years, he stopped competing. Yet, the competitor who lived inside didn't die, it kept eating away at him, trying to break out. Well it wouldn't give up. Somewhere around 1994 it surfaced again and Dick Kirby was compelled to see if he still could win. It became the "Old Guy" as he called himself, against the younger up and coming champs.

Dick prepared himself for "The Grand Nationals" and made it into the finals, which was as he says, "An utterly astonishing accomplishment for me to do."

Dick went into the finals and the M.C. called the first caller up and he began calling. Dick was shocked to discover that somehow in the busyness of the time schedule he was under, he had prepared the wrong calls to do for "The Grand Nationals" finals! "Here is a three minute time segment that people literally spend months and months of practice time on, and I wasn't ready." remembers Dick. Frustrated, he got permission to go outside. In his pockets he searched for any other calls he might have on him. Dick reflects, "I always take all my calls from the preliminary round, put them in a case and get them ready for the next one. When I went outside, in my coat pocket, there were the calls and they were the calls I needed to compete with. Talk about God's providence!" Dick was still very frustrated and thought, "Oh man! I don't want to go up there." As the contest proceeded, caller five went up, caller six went up, caller seven went up. Dick prayed, "Lord I don't want to go up there!" Dick felt a peace come over him as if it was like Jesus put His arm around him and said, "Come on Dick, we'll do this together." With this powerful sense of God's Spirit on him , Dick went forward when his number was called, even though he was totally unprepared. What happened, you ask? Well, here is what Dick said, "I won that contest and it was because of the Lord!"

Dick Kirby is also on the winning side in the battle for the souls of every man, woman and child. Wouldn't you also like to be on the winning side, as all others are cast into "the lake of fire" for ever! For a free booklet on the subject, by Charlie Alsheimer called, "The Ultimate Hunt." Write or call or e-mail us here at God's Great Outdoors and we'll send you a copy along with "The Greatest Hunt of All," by Dwight Schuh too!

"The Great Debate"
#020

When my oldest son, Courtney, was four years old he came to me with what was obvious by the expression on his face, a very serious question. "Daddy, what about the dinosaurs? What does the Bible say about them?" At this point I had been a Christian for almost three years, but still tried to fit evolution into my

Christian thinking. Yet, I was having less peace in my spirit about this approach. You have to really distort God's written word to do this. It was Court's question that made me decide to sort this thing out. So, I told my son, "You know what? I don't know, but I'll find out."

My research quickly had me lay to rest any and all evolutionary ideology I had been hanging onto whatsoever. Despite what secular scientists may state, there are no facts to stand on. Darwin's idea of Natural Selection really doesn't deserve to be called a theory. Interestingly enough, today scientists who hold to Evolution will not debate Creation scientists in public forums, Dr. Kent Hovind has even offered $250,000.00 to anyone who can present scientific proof of Evolution. He has to date no takers (**www.drdino.com).**

One of the best books I have seen to explain creation to both children and adults is *"The Great Dinosaur Mystery And The Bible,"* by Paul S. Taylor (Chariot Family Publishing - A division of Cook Communications). It is an easy to read and informative book that takes you through the book of Job to archaeological discoveries that leave no doubt that God is the Creator who spoke the world into existence. Any questions that may still linger can be laid to rest by contacting Ken Ham and the staff at *Answers-in-Genesis, 1-800-350-3232.* This Creation/teaching based ministry is constantly adding to their scientific material proving Creation, and are a fantastic storehouse of resources for every age group. The video, "Mount St. Helen" by Dr. Steve Austin is also on my "top ten list" of resources. Remember, don't make a bone-headed mistake by trying to hold onto a teaching based on a lie which then will be a road block to receiving Jesus Christ as Creator and Savior of the world.

Hebrews 4:13
"Nothing in all creation is hidden from God's sight. Everything is uncovered and laid bare before the eyes of him to whom we must give account."

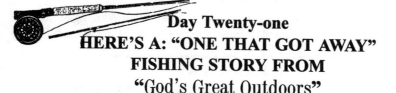

Day Twenty-one
HERE'S A: "ONE THAT GOT AWAY"
FISHING STORY FROM
"God's Great Outdoors"
#023

God's Great Outdoors radio program is, in every way, only on the air because of the Lord's mighty hand. Many people, coupled with numerous events have intertwined together in perfect timing and unison to make this ministry a reality. One of the key individuals in the course of it's development, was Jon Skillman.

Being involved in Christian radio for many years and an outdoorsman who loves time in God's creation, Jon saw the potential for Gerry's idea about an adventure radio ministry and helped him get the program off and flying. Now, about Jon's blunder, well it goes back a few years to say the least. And the event was not something he experienced himself, but was able to observe first hand. It happened on Lake Erie not far off shore from the Sandusky/East Harbor area. In those days, around 1954, when Jon was 8 or 9 years old, this Great Lake was not the fishery it is today. But, still one could expect to catch a fish or two. For this reason Jon's family spent many weekends fishing for bass, walleye or whatever else the waters would produce. The family had rented a fairly substantial boat as size goes for the five fishermen aboard. This gave the group plenty of elbow room. Considering the catch that was about to be made it worked out for the best.

Jon's Uncle Dick, using a live minnow as bait, gave his rod a heave ho and the rig sailed in a high arch. Had it been a punted football, the kicker could have bragged about the hang time. But as the minnow sailed through the air a seagull dropping like a dive bomber, snatched the flying fish in mid air. Like a roped steer it turned into quite a tussle. No one else aboard helped however, as they were all, much too busy laughing their heads off. The air was full of squawking, darting seagull, and sad to say, bad language coming from Jon's uncle. Needless to say, getting the gull unhooked was a real battle.

Now Jon's uncle's biggest blunder wasn't with the seagull, but with the sin nature we are all born with. Jon has won that battle by surrendering his life and heart to Jesus Christ. His uncle, however, well what comes out of the mouth is what is in the heart and many people enter Hell's gates long before they breathe their last breath, metaphorically speaking. In time, Dick's marriage ended, and he drifted off to God only knows where. The family he left behind has been shipwrecked in strife and anger, coming apart too. Now Jon's uncle may have blown it, and maybe your life could be a carbon copy of Dick's, but it doesn't have to end there. To learn how to redirect your life's path and have the fires of Hell removed from your future, e-mail, phone, or write to us here at God's Great Outdoors and we will send you a free copy of "More Than Winning & Losing," by Hank Parker. Plus you will also receive Jim Grassi's, "The Ultimate Fishing Challenge."

HERE'S A:
"MY BIGGEST HUNTING BLUNDER" FROM
"God's Great Outdoors"
#021

The President of *Weatherby Firearms Company* Ed Weatherby, will tell you he has been very blessed. He can point to a number of things to reflect those blessings, one being the many hunting trips with his father when he was a young man. But, one mistake on a hunting trip to Africa could have cost him or one of the hunting party their very lives. Ed had hunted deer, antelope and elk in his home of the USA and pursued plains' game on the Dark Continent as well. The time of this *Blunder* he and his dad were after lions in the country of Kenya.

Now early on that July day, which by the way is the winter on that side of the planet earth, the trackers came upon some lion tracks; they tracked them for a distance, when the Land Rover rounded a bend and there, less than one hundred feet away, were two lions crouched down, with their full attention on the intruders.

Ed remembers, "My initial reaction (or instinct) as I've always done was to bail out of the vehicle and chamber a round in my rifle. I was going to shoot the lion, because of course that's what we were there for. Just about the time I was about to pull the trigger, I heard all this commotion behind me." The professional hunter had assessed the situation instantly and reacted as quickly. He scrambled to the top of the Land Rover, rifle in hand while Ed squeezed off a shot to down one of the big cats. The second beast was hit almost before the young Ed Weatherby could pull the trigger on the lion he had set his sights on. Immediately Ed's thoughts were, "This is rather odd?"

What Ed in his young years, and lack of experience with this dangerous of a quarry did not realize, is that the two lions were less than two seconds, or in other words, just two quick leaps away from attacking either Ed or the group. Shares Ed, "I was outside the vehicle which, number one, I was not supposed to have done. Number two, the trackers were now in the rear of the vehicle which was open completely, exposing them, and the lions could have attacked them. So, I felt pretty stupid as a 17 year old kid in how I hunted." Therefore, to protect the entire hunting party, the professional hunter had to dispatch the accompanying lion, before it had time to react to Ed's mistake.

Ed Weatherby may have "jumped the gun" so to speak, on that hunt for lion, but one place he did not jump too quickly, and that's when it comes to his personal relationship with the Savior Jesus Christ. God's word says Satan is like a roaring lion seeking whom ever he can devour. Why not defeat the enemy's plan and be assured of everlasting life with the Creator God? For a free booklet to help you called, "The Ultimate Hunt," by Charlie Alsheimer, contact us here at God's Great Outdoors by phone, mail, or e-mail and we'll get one to you. In fact we will also send "The Greatest Hunt of All," by Dwight Schuh along as well.

"Why?"
#021

As an unbeliever, one aspect of the Bible I had a problem believing was in the area of Jesus' last night before the crucifixion. In the Gospel of Luke, this physician related how Jesus, while praying, had sweat like drops of blood falling to the ground. This seemed to me, more impossible than even the miracles. However, there truly is a medical phenomenon known as hematidrosis. Under extremely great emotional stress, tiny capillaries in the sweat glands can burst and mix with sweat. The process makes the person weak, the skin becomes fragile and tender, additionally, shock is a possibility. Then after a sleepless night, dehydrated, blindfolded, mocked, spat upon and struck in the face with their fists, the palace guards hand Jesus over to the Romans. These soldiers stripped him of his clothing, tying his hands to a post above his head in preparation for the flogging. The tool used was a short whip consisting of several heavy leather thongs with small lead balls at the end and pieces of sheep bones tied at intervals. The soldier began his task with great force. The whip struck Jesus repeatedly across the shoulders, back, buttocks, and legs.

After first cutting through the skin, continued blows cut deeper into subcutaneous tissues. Oozing blood escapes from damaged capillaries and veins in outer layers. Bleeding increased as underlying muscles were reached. The lead balls worked to produce deep bruises, breaking open with later blows, his skin hanging in ribbons, Jesus' back is a torn, bleeding, unrecognizable mass of meat. Sometimes these whippings could expose rib bones and even sections of the spinal column. The idea here was not to kill, only to weaken the criminal to just short of collapse.

With this torture over, the Romans untied Jesus and threw a purple robe on His shoulders, a stick representing a king's scepter was put in his hands and a crown made of thorns pushed into his scalp. After jesting and striking Him, they ripped the cloak off, causing agonizing pain as the wounds which had clotted to the cloth material reopened. Then, if that wasn't enough, next came the Creator of the world's crucifixion.

John 1:10
"He was in the world, and though the world was made through him, the world did not recognize him."

John 15:13
"Greater love has no one than this, that he lay down his life for his friends."

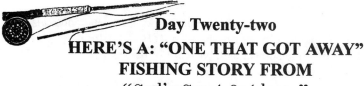

Day Twenty-two
HERE'S A: "ONE THAT GOT AWAY"
FISHING STORY FROM
"God's Great Outdoors"
#024

When the words "wedding ring" are mentioned, the picture that first comes to most minds is the groom slipping a band of gold onto his beautiful bride's finger. But, to many diehard fisherman in the northwest, the picture is of a fishing lure darting through a pristine mountain stream or lake. The *Mack's Lure* Company's arsenal includes this regionally popular artificial bait. Don Talbot is the company's marketing manager, so you might think his days are spent fishing, but that's just not the case. However, when Don does get the chance to fish, he jumps on it. Sometimes squeezing two fishing trips into one.

Such is the case in Don's fishing fiasco. He and his friend had spent the morning fishing for Steelhead on the Columbia River. Their trolling efforts yielded only one fish which took it's place in the cooler. But, as the day wore on, the pair loaded the boat and headed toward home. Yet, the fishing bug that bites had not been fully fed, so they planned a stop on the way. The destination of the second leg was the high mountain and still very frozen Banks Lake in the center of Washington, to do some ice fishing. The problem was that the February winds picked up strength as they made their way from the Washington-Oregon border where the Columbia River flows.

Now the anglers had just tossed all the equipment in the boat, never giving it a second thought. As they whizzed down the highway they reached an area where the winds's power was being multiplied by the funneling effect of a mountain pass the vehicle was traveling through. Unbeknownst to them, all their gear was starting to go airborne and the highway was becoming littered as they moved on. They only realized this about the time everything in the boat had been blown out. So, the two began to back track to recover all their stuff. Not sure where it had been lost, a green jar of bait caught the eye of this search and rescue team as it lay just off the road's surface. This began the half mile trail of blown out fishing tackle they recovered from the roadways. Ninety percent of the equipment was found, including rods & reels, power baits and such. Even a filet knife, which when it blew out had stuck, blade first, in the dirt next to the road was found. But as for the ten percent still lost, Don says, "Some of it, who knows where it went."

Don Talbot may have lost some of his gear forever, but as for his position after death, he's not lost there, but locked in for eternity. Don has given Jesus Christ, the One who is searching and is the only rescue, an open door to his heart. His name will be found and forever in the Lamb's Book of Life. Yours can be too! To learn more on the subject call, write, or e-mail us here at God's Great Outdoors to receive a free copy of "More Than Winning & Losing," by Hank Parker and you will also receive a copy of Jim Grassi's, "The Ultimate Fishing Challenge."

HERE'S A:
"MY BIGGEST HUNTING BLUNDER" FROM
"God's Great Outdoors"
#022
Written By Dave Watson and Edited For Radio Broadcast By Gerry Caillouet

As the host and producer of *Bushnell's Secrets Of The Hunt* on TNN, Dave Watson has the opportunity to bowhunt in some fine locations. Dave starts, "Folks think us 'pros' no longer make silly mistakes, but believe me, we definitely do! Let me tell you about a very embarrassing one."

"I was hunting in Alberta and the snow covered ground was covered with fresh deer tracks. I placed my API treestand downwind from the trail in hopes at least one set of tracks belonged to a big buck. As the sun rose the next morning, I had been sitting there with my safety belt on for at least an hour. Everything was perfect - the wind, the foliage behind me to hide my silhouette, everything! My experience has taught me to hang all gear in the tree within easy reach and there was a tree to my right that would serve that purpose perfectly. Screw-in hooks from my backpack held my arrow quiver and my deer call. The deer call has a convenient lanyard that most people hang around their necks, but I've found this may cause some extra noise and noise is not a good thing for a bowhunter. Thirty minutes after sunrise, I saw him," Dave continues. "A hundred yards away was a beautiful 8 point buck and he had my name on him! Yep, right there on his side said, 'DAVE'S BUCK' in flashing neon. He was mine! I reached over with my right hand and grasped the call. I slowly raised it to my lips and blew softly. 'Ehhhh, Ehhhhh.' The buck immediately began walking towards me! 80 yards, 70 yards, he stopped at 60 yards, so I blew softly once again. 'Ehhhh, Ehhhh.' Now he was coming for sure! At 40 yards his head was hidden behind a thick clump of willows, this was my chance. I gently let the call swing back next to the tree still hanging by the hook, but when I started to put my release on my bow string, I felt some resistance. My eyes darted to my hand. The lanyard was hopelessly tangled around my release! The lanyard looked like it had earned badges for an entire troop of Boy Scouts. The buck walked by me at 18 yards broadside and I couldn't take the shot!

"Back at the cabin, my friend asked me how I did. 'A big 8 point came by at 18 yards,' I said. 'Why didn't you shoot him?' I just said, 'Well, I was all tied up at the time.'"

Dave Watson may have been unprepared on that hunt, but one place where Dave is prepared is when it comes to meeting his Creator and Lord Jesus Christ. You also can find success in the ultimate of hunts, the one for eternal salvation. Contact us by mail, phone or e-mail here at God's Great Outdoors for a free booklet by Charlie Alsheimer called, "The Ultimate Hunt." We'll also send along "The Greatest Hunt of All," by Dwight Schuh.

"Creation Crushes Creator"
#022

The invention of crucifixion is traced first to the Persians, but it is the Romans who perfected this tortuous means of execution. So agonizing is this method of death they had to invent a word just to describe the painful experience. *Excruciating* means "out of the cross." Jesus not only was to die on the cross, He also had to carry it to the place of execution. Imagine, after the beating He had received, having to carry a beam weighing seventy-five to one hundred and twenty-five pounds on those mangled shoulders. Not long after they started, Jesus stumbled, fell and His load was passed on to a bystander to carry. When the procession arrived at Golgotha (The Place of the Skull), Jesus was thrown back against the cross beam. Then, tapered iron spikes, approximately six inches long, were driven in the wrists on each end of the timber. The soldier lifted the cross piece into place and the feet, one on top of the other, were placed on the upright post with knees bent and a nail driven in through the arches. As Jesus pushed upward to avoid the stretching torment on His arms, He had to place full weight on the nail in His feet. Soon, the arms fatigued and powerful waves of cramps swept His muscles, they knotted, causing constant pain. These cramps caused difficulty in pushing up. Hanging by the arms paralyzed the chest muscles resulting in the rib muscles' inability to function. Thus, Jesus could draw air into His lungs, but exhalation was not possible. So, He would have had to fight to lift himself up in order to catch a short breath. Once carbon dioxide levels had built up in the lungs and the bloodstream, the cramping would have subsided partially. With spasmodic movements Jesus pushed Himself upwards to inhale and exhale each time He breathed.

The time was filled with limitless, fiery pain, constant muscle cramps throughout the body, asphyxiation combined with the agonizing action of scraping His torn backside on the rough timber in the act of gaining a life giving breath. Then a tight squeezing pain starts deep in the chest as the pericardium begins to fill with serum, compressing the heart. Straining upward one last time, Jesus who had already asked His Father to forgive those who had committed this atrocity, cried out, "It is finished!" and died.

Some of the criminals who were crucified lived up to four days. Included in this tortuous event were insects landing on or burrowing into open wounds, eyes, ears or the nose. Also, birds of prey and vultures would tear at these locations. Yet, Jesus and His death was unlike any other, for this was God in the flesh, the Creator who went to the cross for every man, woman, and child. To pay for their sins, if only they will receive Him and His sacrifice. If you receive Him, you will be with Him for eternity, because three days after His death, He arose from the dead and ascended to be with the Father in Heaven.

John 3:16,17
"For God so loved the world that he gave his one and only Son, that whoever believes in him shall not perish but have eternal life. For God did not send his Son into the world to condemn the world, but to save the world through him."

Day Twenty-three
HERE'S A: "ONE THAT GOT AWAY"
FISHING STORY FROM
"God's Great Outdoors"
#025

Brent Jones is rather a newcomer to the world of fishing. These days, he is able to spend more of his time angling and his skill level shows that, but for years much of each year was dedicated to his profession, football. This tight end played for the *San Francisco Forty-Niners* helping them win three Super Bowl victories, and it is in the midst of this career that his blunder occurred. Brent, who was accompanied by his father-in-law and two high school buddies, was in a hurry as the group hiked through "Gold Country" to the Mokelmne River in an area near Jackson, California.

The air temperature was in the fifties that spring morning. The crispness of the dawning day, coupled with the mountainous country, messed together with the excitement of what lurked under the water's surface, making it hard for Brent to control his anticipation. Brent states, "I had a new Panther Martin lure I'd bought and I couldn't tie it on fast enough. Mine was the first line in the water!"

Now Brent's two friends were much more experienced than he, and they both were fishing with live bait. They put little store in artificials, so what happened next is no surprise. On his first cast, Brent had the biggest strike of his life as a seven to eight pound Rainbow trout hooked on. He remembers, "My pole almost snapped, but both my friends thought I was snagged and they began to laugh and make fun of me." They were fishing further on down the river and from their position could not see the huge trout that Brent had hooked into. However, the fight lasted less than ten seconds as Brent had failed to tie his new lure on properly.

To add fuel to the fire, his cronies, who thought worms were the only way to go, watched as their less knowledgeable comrade tied on another "fake bait" identical to the first. Brent cast to the same area and again on his first cast, the lure was slammed! As he fought this fish, his ex-school mates broke out in laughter, thinking he had again hooked on the bottom. However, their fun lasted only about thirty seconds as a four pound Rainbow exploded out of the water before their very eyes. The sudden silence was broken only by the sound of four feet running on the gravel covered river bed as they both dropped everything and rushed to help their chum land his catch.

Now Brent Jones blew it when it came to tying on the first line and he lost the bigger Rainbow trout, but God gave him a second chance to prove his angling ability. However, Brent knew that we get no second chance after death to receive Jesus Christ and be saved from the eternal fires of Hell, and neither will you. To learn more on the subject of life everlasting in the midst of peace and joy, write, e-mail, or call us at God's Great Outdoors and we will send you a free copy of Hank Parker's, "More Than Winning & Losing," plus you will also get a copy of "The Ultimate Fishing Challenge," by Jim Grassi.

HERE'S A:
"MY BIGGEST HUNTING BLUNDER" FROM
"God's Great Outdoors"
Written By T.R. Michels And Edited For Radio Broadcast By Gerry Caillouet
#023

Outdoors writer, seminar speaker and professional hunting guide, T.R. Michels, begins sharing about his hunting blunder by reflecting on how many he has had. T.R. states, "I don't know how many hunting blunders I've made in my life, several dozen at least. Some blunders cost me a shot, others got me wet and cold, like the time I fell in a duck slough. It happened while I was trying to pull my foot out of the muck. Thank God the slough was shallow and it was a fairly warm day.

I was soaked to the neck, both my hip boots were full of water and I had duck-weed pouring out of the barrel of my shotgun. If the ducks hadn't been flying overhead it might have been funny. That's what most of my blunders were like, just inconveniences."

T.R. continues, "The blunder that could have cost the most momentarily occurred while I was turkey hunting in southern Minnesota. When I got back to my Blazer, I found that I'd locked my keys inside. Chewing myself out for being an idiot I took off my turkey vest, put my gun down and tried to figure out how I could break into the truck. I could see the keys still in the ignition, so close, yet so far. Silently I prayed, 'Lord, please let someone come and help me.' As I tried to figure out what to do, it hit me. I took out my Coleman knife and jimmied the latch on the vent window. I was grateful I had a slight build as I squeezed my arm through the window and grasped the keys. When I finally had the door open I said, 'Thank you Lord.'

"It wasn't until after I got home and began to unload the truck that I discovered I had forgotten my gun. I told my wife what I had done and got back in the truck. Chewing myself out, I started praying again, 'Lord, please don't let anyone see my gun, and please let it still be there.' I couldn't remember exactly where I had put the gun, so I stopped the truck a short way from where I had first parked. I looked in the grass on both sides of where I had parked but couldn't find the gun. I was sure I had left it on the ground near the driver side door.

"I looked around one more time and was ready to put the truck in gear when I saw it." Leaning against the tree directly in front of the truck was his firearm. Once more he thanked God. The gun was in plain view and not five yards off the road. But, because the gun was camouflaged, it was almost impossible to see. "Some people might call this a lucky experience" adds T.R., "I call it being looked after by a very loving Father, God."

"My faith in God has taught me to look at the blunders, mistakes, accidents and disasters in my life differently than some people might. When things went wrong before, I might have thought it couldn't get worse. Now that I have accepted Jesus as my Lord and Savior, I see that things could have been much worse."

One may wonder how much worse than not finding his turkey gun could it be? Well, T.R. Michels found something far more valuable than anything we can own. When he placed his trust in the Savior, Jesus Christ, he received the greatest gift anyone can receive, eternal life. You can also find assurance of life everlasting. To learn more, write, e-mail, or call God's Great Outdoors for a free copy of "The Ultimate Hunt," by Charlie Alsheimer. We will also send Dwight Schuh's, "The Greatest Hunt of All."

"Out of the Deep"
#023

Here is a stranger than fiction true story I pulled off the wire service some years ago. It is one of the most amazing true stories I have ever heard. It started when officials discovered a deceased man dressed in a full wetsuit, with dive tank, face mask, and flippers. The scuba diver was found not floating on the water or on some beach, but inland in a burned out area of a California forest. After an autopsy, it was determined that the diver had not died from burns, but massive internal injuries.

Once a positive identification was made on the man, investigators made a startling discovery. They found out that the frogman had been diving in the vast Pacific Ocean, some twenty kilometers from where he was found in the smoldering, but distinguished, charred forest remains. It was determined that when a fleet of helicopters were called in to aid fire fighters, and they began dropping very large buckets into the ocean, more than just sea water was picked-up. Rapidly filling these water containers, the choppers rushed to the flaming forest to dump their load of water on to the fire. The diver who was scooped up out of the great expanses of the Pacific, then plunged to his death when the helicopters arrived at the burning tree tops and opened the buckets to try and dowse the inferno.

This is a true story and you can be sure that the man on that day and in that way, never thought for one moment he would not see tomorrow because of such a freak accident. His thoughts for the day's trip may have included worries about the proper amount of oxygen in his tank, the regulator's function, or sharks in that area. No one would have listed this as a danger to give even one moment's concern.

Do you know if you will have a tomorrow, if not, and you died this moment, could you say beyond a shadow of a doubt you would stand in the presence of God? If not, trust in Jesus Christ today as you may not have a tomorrow to wait upon.

Psalm 103:15-18
"As for man, his days are like grass, he flourishes like a flower of the field; the wind blows over it and it is gone, and its place remembers it no more. But from everlasting to everlasting the Lord's love is with those who fear him, and his righteousness with their children's children— with those who keep his covenant and remember to obey his precepts."

James 4:13,14
"Now listen, you who say, 'Today or tomorrow we will go to this or that city, spend a year there, carry on business and make money.' Why, you do not even know what will happen tomorrow. What is your life? You are a mist that appears for a little while and then vanishes."

Chapter Twenty-four
HERE'S A: "ONE THAT GOT AWAY"
FISHING STORY FROM
"God's Great Outdoors"
#026

Now in the later years of his life, though he is by no means idle, Ron Lindner has the time to put into some of the "crafty ideas" he had to shelve years ago. Those inventive tackle projects were put aside because Ron and his brother Al, were so very busy with *In-Fisherman*. From the magazine to the television show, radio, video, books, seminars and the list goes on and on, the time just would not allow for everything. So, the more important and necessary things won out. But in the beginning of Ron's journey in the fishing business world, those crafty inventions were his bread and butter. His maiden voyage was in fishing tackle manufacturing, with his and Al's own *Lindy Tackle Company* which set sail in the '60's.

In the early days of this fledgling manufacturer, they would do promos at various locations to show how their fishing tackle performed. Ron remembers, "Running hand to mouth, breakdowns happened often as we had nothing new and beautiful in the way of equipment to do our promotions with. We'd have no spare spark plugs, develop a problem, and have to go back to buy one." But Ron's biggest boo-boo when it comes to fishing fiascos comes when he was in the process of setting up to do one of the promotional events. The promo setting was on Clear Lake in Iowa, on a very cold and windy day. Now it had been heavily advertised, so there was a small gathering of people despite the chilly conditions. Ron and crew arriving before the program was to start, backed to the dock and launched the boat. Tying the water craft to the dock, the car and trailer were then parked. A glance at the vessel brought a shock to Ron's being, it was filling with water! In fact, it was half full! Dressed as he was, not for scuba diving, he jumped into the boat and began the desperate search for the plug in the rear of the boat. Someone else raced to the family vehicle to back it to the dock, but it wouldn't start and had to be jumped. When Ron found the plug by feeling around in the murky water, his hand numb with cold, combined with being anxious to screw it in, caused... well the chain holding the plug to break and Ron dropped the plug. Unable to find it again as it drifted off underwater, he desperately jumped in to the lake's water and pushed the craft up as far as possible on the boat ramp. Eventually the car was started, some water emptied and the craft loaded onto the trailer to kind of finish the drying process. With the plug found and inserted, Ron reflects, "I've never forgotten to check the plug from that day on."

Ron Lindner may have been absentminded in relation to the boat's drain plug that cold and windy day in Iowa, but there is one place where he had his thinking on a solid foundation, and that was on the Rock, Christ Jesus. Ron is standing on the Lord for eternity in looking toward Heaven and you can be too. Want to know more? E-mail, phone, or write us here at God's Great Outdoors for Hank Parker's "More Than Winning & Losing." Plus we'll send "The Ultimate Fishing Challenge," by Jim Grassi and both of these are free!

HERE'S A:
"MY BIGGEST HUNTING BLUNDER" FROM
"God's Great Outdoors"
Adapted From Russell Thornberry's Book, *BUCKS, BULLS & BELLY LAUGHS* And Edited For Radio Broadcast By Gerry Caillouet
#024

For many years, before he became the Executive Editor of *Buckmaster Magazine*, Russell Thornberry made his living as a outfitter and guide in the Canadian province of Alberta. Here's just one of his moose hunter mishaps.

In late September of 1974, Russell was walking a client through a black spruce muskeg and began calling for a bull moose. After twenty minutes he decided to move to a new location when he heard what sounded like the beating of large wings approaching through the still silent air. Yet looking up, Russell did not see a bird in the sky. The sound grew louder and then in the timber ahead movement caught his eye. "Before I could comment," remembers Russ, "a pack of wolves were standing in a semi-circle around us. The sound had been the panting of the running wolves. It all happened so quickly that it seemed almost imaginary."

The wolves realizing that the hunters were not moose, but humans, simply faded away. Surprised, but not fearful, Russ had learned over the years how much wolves fear and avoid man. His hunter was not convinced about their innocence, he turned white as a sheet and kept looking over his shoulder all day long.

Well, two days later with only 30 minutes of shooting light left, Russ and his hunter had climbed on top of a pile of dead trees to hide from the view of any approaching moose. Russell called to any bull moose who might be nearby. It was getting dark when they both heard a branch snap behind them. Bull moose will sometimes tiptoe in so the hunter got ready. Waiting and straining to listen, the two heard nothing when out of thin air, a huge black bear suddenly reared up on it's hind legs. Only six feet away the hunter screamed in horror and fired a

85

shot in the air. The bear vanished and the hunter danced a jig of uncontrollable nervous tension while half crying and half laughing. This had shaken him deeply and nothing Russ said convinced him the wolf and the bear incidents were once in a lifetime type events.

The bull moose that finally did get called in for this hunter, sneaked in like a mouse. The hunter who was sitting against a stump one hundred yards from Russell, did not see the bull directly behind him, some fifteen feet away. With both of them looking his way, Russ could do nothing but sit still. Eventually, the moose stepped on a piece of dead wood that cracked under his feet and sounded like an explosion. The poor hunter came off of the ground as if fired from a cannon, turned and fired a wild shot, which missed the bull, but whirled him in a circle of confusion. Then they stood ten feet away eyeballing each other. After an eternity, the hunter shot. Russ says,"Both the moose and hunter dropped in unison, the moose dead and the hunter fainted. He finally got himself together and he could only describe the termination of his hunt as pure relief." Russell too once was on a hunt that ended in pure relief. The hunt for eternal salvation through Jesus Christ. You also can find this ultimate peace. For a free booklet on the subject by Charles Alsheimer, titled "The Ultimate Hunt," contact us at God's Great Outdoors by mail, phone, or e-mail and you'll also receive "The Greatest Hunt of All," by Dwight Schuh.

"I Owe, I Owe So Off To Work I Go!"
#024

The pastor of my home church has used an illustration several times during the years that our family has attended Community Grace Brethren Church in West Milton, Ohio. Pastor Steve Peters makes the point that if the newspaper headlines read something like this, *"WAY TO HEAVEN DISCOVERED!,"* people would be enthralled with the article if it was something they could do. He relates, if the story went on to explain how it was determined that anyone who crawled on their hands and knees from the Atlantic Ocean to the Pacific Ocean would be guaranteed a place in Heaven, one thing is sure–the roads would be filled, crowded even with people on their hands and knees struggling to make it across our continent. When I interviewed Matt McPherson at the *Mathews Inc.* factory in Sparta, Wisconsin, he shared a similar insight. Matt related that never in all the times he had asked a similar question, did he receive a negative response. When asked if hanging on a cross everyday of one's life, from nine-to-five would make it possible for the person to spend eternity in Heaven, and would it be worth it? "Yes!," was always the answer. But what can we do to be assured of life everlasting with God? Nothing!

You must understand everything we might do will fall short, miss the mark and cause us, in the end, to be ushered into the Lake of Fire with Satan and his demonic followers. There is good news however! It is not what *we* do, but what *Jesus* did! He paid the price for our sins - past, present and future. I have had some say to me, "I'll become a Christian, but first I must...." stop this or that thing in their life. Friend, you don't take a shower to get clean before a bath! Jesus shed blood on the cross did it all, just receive Him as Savior. He'll clean you up, to be sure.

Romans 6:23
"For the wages of sin is death, but the gift of God is eternal life in Christ Jesus, our Lord"

Ephesians 2:8,9
"For it is by grace you have been saved, through faith—and this not from yourselves, it is the gift of God—not by works, so that no one can boast."

Day Twenty-five
HERE'S A: "ONE THAT GOT AWAY" FISHING STORY FROM
"God's Great Outdoors"
#027

The only career professional bass fisherman Joe Thomas has known is, well, tournament fishing. Joe pushes himself very hard, that is why he has been able to stay at it so long; that's a part of winning. Another key to his success is the pre-fishing which helps him get to know the waters he'll be competing on. It was on one of those pre-fishing outings where Joe almost lost his life because of a simple accident.

It was 1985 and Joe was involved in the actual "official" pre-fishing. He was fishing on the Mississippi River near La Cross, Wisconsin and was out early on that cold and clear autumn morning. A slight mist of fog hung above the warmer water as the chilly air came in contact with the rapidly moving current. As Joe motored along he swung his boat into position in the faster flow near the dam's base and lowered the trolling motor. Beginning to cast into the swift moving water, Joe worked the area with the hopes of finding a hot spot to hit when the tournament got under way. He was standing in the front of his office - the bass boat, when the fast current caught the water craft and swung it sideways. The vessel then hit a floating log which lunged the boat back, throwing Joe off balance and into the fifty degree water. The snow mobile suit which had worked so well to combat the forty degree air temperature, was now loaded down with water. This made staying afloat tough, let alone swimming. But Joe realized the bass boat was moving away and made his best effort to reach it before his strength gave out. He was able to grab the trolling motor's shaft for some much needed rest. Then he worked to the rear of the boat and with all the energy he had left, worked himself back aboard the boat.

Some nine years later, in 1994, Joe had a vision of what might have been on the Mississippi River that morning years before. While unofficially pre-fishing in New York's 1000 Islands area, he, a friend and his friend's eleven-year old son made a gruesome discovery. The group was fishing on a chilly September morning, as a cold front had pushed the temperature to thirty degrees that morning. The three were casting to the shore with the boat in ten to twelve feet of water, when the clear water below suddenly revealed a man's body below the surface. Since they were fishing the Canada side, the Mounties were contacted. The officials on recovering the drowning victim found he had ended his own life by tying a concrete block to his leg. Joe had looked into the face of this dead man and saw someone who had given up - Joe had chosen not to. You see Joe knows he not only wins because of hard work, but because God has a plan for everyone's life. Joe Thomas discovered this plan began when he asked Jesus Christ to be his Lord and Savior and you can too. To learn more, contact us here at God's Great Outdoors and we will send you a free copy of "More Than Winning & Losing," by Hank Parker. You will also receive Jim Grassi's "The Ultimate Fishing Challenge."

HERE'S A:
"MY BIGGEST HUNTING BLUNDER" FROM
"God's Great Outdoors"
#025

Paul Meeks, the President and owner of *API Outdoors Inc.*'s hunting blunder flashes before his eyes time and time again. Why? Because it happened while he and a team from API Outdoors were shooting a segment for a treestand safety video. Paul reflects, "Having my hunting mistake caught on film makes it worse. Up close and personal."

They were hunting in Goliad, Texas on a beautiful, bright, sunny day at the end of October. In fact, it was a perfect day and for that matter, it was perfect conditions to be shooting video footage of a hunt. But, alas in all that perfectness, something can go wrong. As you see we live in a world suffering from the effects of sin.

Paul was sitting in his treestand with a cameraman in another stand behind him. A white tail buck, a real trophy buck entered the scene feeding toward the elevated pair. Paul was not nervous or suffering from the effects of buck fever. He calmly waited and gave his cameraman plenty of time to get ready for the upcoming action. Paul, with a sign that his cameraman was ready, set himself to make the shot. The deer was within easy bow range as Paul pulled his bow back and anchored, holding to give the cameraman time to make any adjustments. The buck for some unknown reason raised his head and looked straight at him. Paul states, "When a deer looks at you in Texas more than any other place, it seems you'll miss as he drops under the arrow." Yet, Paul decided to let the arrow fly. The buck's back dropped as he prepared to bound away thus the arrow flew over the deer's back.

Paul remembers, "His back dropped 14 to 18 inches. A genuine trophy, purely typical 8 point, 20-22 inch spread, perfectly symmetrical with 6 to 8 inch bow tines. I had him right there at 18 yards. I had him already hanging on the wall. We later estimated he'd go 150 Pope & Young points. He was a record buck!" But all Paul got was an education and on video too.

Now Paul Meeks may not have put that buck in the record book, but there is one book Paul is in, and that is the book that determines his place for all of eternity, The Lamb's Book of Life. Is your name in that book? To end your search for eternal peace, contact God's Great Outdoors by mail, phone, or e-mail for a free booklet by Charles Alsheimer, called "The Ultimate Hunt." We will send a copy of "The Greatest Hunt of All," by Dwight Schuh.

"Ready-Aim-Fire!"
#025

For fifteen years, I worked on the big car haulers that drove across our nation and Canada hauling the new cars to dealership car lots. The factory my terminal serviced as an auto manufacturers sub-contractor was near my home. This particular plant first produced pick-up trucks. Later, it was tooled over to another type of vehicle. I was working second shift at the time when this incident happened and I had been called in that Monday, two hours early. As I welded on the trailer on one of those big seventy-five foot vehicles, one of my co-workers arrived at the normal shift starting time.

Now my stand for Jesus was no secret and I had taken an assortment of hits, if you will, over the years. It comes with the territory, Christ Jesus told the disciples this would happen and not to be concerned. So, when I asked the unsaved fella how his weekend had been, he responded with a kind of teasing, but serious remark, as we had a good, friendly relationship. "You don't want to know Gerry, 'cause I sinned all weekend!" My response was quick and to the point, "Well good for you, if I were you I would sin like crazy, a mad man even! There isn't anything I wouldn't do, because after you die, it's all down hill for you and this is the best you'll ever have. Kind of your only taste of heaven. So, why not give it all the gusto you've got man, because it doesn't get any better than this. Unless you become a Christian, it's all over and Hell is your final destination." Well, he had been toying with me and never expected that kind of response. He stormed off and didn't speak to me for two days, but the truth was out there.

I had made this comment out of true concern for my co-workers eternal position. I knew this man and had shared the Gospel's truth numerous times with him. He had read the Bible through and I had prayed for him for a long time. I believe that one day he will receive Jesus as Lord and Savior. It is all in God's perfect timing. I also think God brought to mind what needed to be said in a way he needed to hear it, and he can't say I didn't tell him either. Here is the question, where are you?

Ecclesiastes 7:20
"There is not a righteous man on earth who does what is right and never sins."

Romans 10:17
"Consequently, faith comes from hearing the message, and the message is heard, through the word of Christ."

Day Twenty-six
HERE'S A: "ONE THAT GOT AWAY"
FISHING STORY FROM
"God's Great Outdoors"
#028

When asked for a fishing blunder, Bill Dance host of *Bill Dance's Outdoors*, commented that he could "do a show on blunders and foul ups every week!" But the one Bill focused on was the most fearful outing he'd ever had, as it was only by the grace of God he survived that mistake.

Years ago he was fishing a very large body of water in Mexico. Bill and his friend had flown in the day before the camera crew was due to arrive with the fishing boats. Instead of taking the time to just kick back and relax, the pair decided to rent a boat from some locals at the camp they were using as a base of operation on this particular television project. Bill reflects, "The rentals looked like hollowed out bananas. We took one with an outboard and went up the lake. A major storm hit. It was perhaps the most scared that I've ever been in my life." Their attempt to race back before the storm slammed into them, failed. Bill continues, "I knew in my mind with the waves and the size of the boat we were in real trouble. Then the outboard quit, the steering broke lose, it was bad." Bill's friend had to work the fifty horse engine to steer by hand as Bill got the engine running and worked the throttle gingerly to keep the motor running. Bill says, "It became so bad I literally saw my funeral, I saw myself lying in a casket. I saw my family, my wife and kids standing beside me. I actually saw myself lying there looking up at 'em! I knew my time was up. I can't even exaggerate how bad the situation was, it was almost dark. It was just a foolish, stupid thing we did! The boy with me, I had never heard him pray in his life, he turned and said, 'I can swim, but not that distance and in this type of water as far out as we are. The waves are so bad we're not going to make it.' So I shouted back, 'Pray!'" Bill was not passing on counsel that he was not applying to himself. "I was saying them as fast as I could say them, that got us through it. We managed to break into a pocket....we were full of water, the motor was just about out - gone. It was an experience I'll never forget. I know the Good Lord was with us, He's the best fishing partner I've got, and He was riding with us that day, there's no question," concludes Bill.

Now Bill Dance may have made a judgement error by going out that day in such shaky equipment, but he's not on shaky ground when it comes to how he's geared for eternal life, he's placed his feet on the Solid Rock, Christ Jesus and you don't have to be tossed in the storms of life either. To have your position locked in for good, write, call or e-mail us here at God's Great Outdoors for a free booklet by Hank Parker called, "More Than Winning & Losing." You will also receive Jim Grassi's "The Ultimate Fishing Challenge."

HERE'S A:
"MY BIGGEST HUNTING BLUNDER" FROM
"God's Great Outdoors"
#026

Besides founding the ministry of, *"Let's Go Fishing,"* Jim Grassi, ex-pro bass fisherman, also likes to go afield to hunt big game animals. But as we all know, things don't always go right. In fact, Jim Grassi's hunting blunder almost cost him his life.

Jim was hunting in the top of New Zealand's Alpine Mountains. His quarry was the transplanted Himalayan Tahr. The Tahr is a goat-like animal which closely resembles a miniature North American Buffalo. These agile creatures are tough to find and even tougher to hunt.

Jim was in the middle of a fact finding mission and only had a few days to hunt. Despite an uneasy feeling about the prospective hunt, Jim had gone with the group anyway. The guide loaded him and three other hunters aboard a helicopter and flew them deep into the Alpine Mountains.

Having landed, scouted, and deciding to move to a new area, the guide told Jim to keep his rifle loaded and hold it outside of the chopper. Not liking the idea, Jim followed orders, but held the firearm a little too high. The barrel's muzzle nicked the rotor blade and created the risk of an imbalance. They had to shut the rotor engine off. Neither the radio or the cellular phone could contact the outside world as they were in a box canyon. With night approaching and very cold temperatures expected which none of them were prepared for, they elected to hike down off the mountain top. With only two small pen lights, the men descended steep drop-offs in heavy brush. They risked putting out an eye or worse, falling to their deaths in the dark. At 3 am, a rescue helicopter located them and ended their dangerous trek.

Jim shares, "Man will fail you, equipment will fail you, God is still there. Even if we fail one another, God's direction will guide us through."

Jim might have almost lost it there, but one place he didn't lose it was when it comes to his eternal life with our God and Savior Jesus Christ. For a free booklet by Charlie Alsheimer called, "The Ultimate Hunt," contact us here at God's Great Outdoors by mail, phone, or e-mail. We will also send you "The Greatest Hunt of All," by Dwight Schuh.

"Marching To A Different Drummer"
#026

When my particular jobs would allow, I always played my radio tuned to Christian stations in the shop's bay where I worked as a diesel mechanic/welder on car haulers. I was careful not to have it loud enough to be a bother to others, despite their boxes booming out Country, Oldies or Rock-n-Roll. But considering the content of the radio waves I was interrupting, someone was bound to notice the difference.

One day as I repaired a hydraulic valve locked in a vise, another mechanic came strolling past my radio as it played some music. He commented on how every time he came down where I worked, it sounded like Christmas music or something to that effect. Now, he was just making conversation and had not meant a cut in any way. But, I used the opportunity to point out a spiritual truth. In a matter of fact manner, I said, "That's just the way it will be one day for all of us. Either Christmas music all the time or wailing and gnashing of teeth. You can take your pick!" His reply took on a more serious tone, "I'm sorry I said anything!" I responded, "Well it's a fact, clearly pointed out in God's word, I just wanted to be sure you understood that." With that he trotted off saying, "Ok, you told me!" In later years he would listen a little, but he always had his own ideas and even more important things going on, such as the cares of life and recreational activities.

If someone is turned-off to God because "some pesky" Christians keep telling them the truth, even if they don't want to hear it, sorry. All I can say is that it is our God-given task, it's known as *The Great Commission*. The marching orders are from Jesus Christ Himself, and understand this, Jesus spoke of Hell and judgment more than He talked of Heaven. Why? Simply because He came to save the sinners by giving His life as a ransom for sins, one and all. If you will only put down the excuses and ask Him to come into your heart, you will be saved. Why not ask yourself, what music will you hear for eternity?

Romans 10:13
"Everyone who calls on the name of the Lord will be saved."

2 Corinthians 5:10
"For we must all appear before the judgment seat of Christ, that each one may receive what is due him for the things done while in the body, whether good or bad."

Day Twenty-seven
HERE'S A: "ONE THAT GOT AWAY"
FISHING STORY FROM
"God's Great Outdoors"
#029

If you're involved in archery and you're not aware of the innovative development in compound bows known as the *Solo-Cam*, well you must have your head in the sand. This single cam invention has taken the professional archery shooting world by storm, and needless to say, the bowhunting community is also turning over to this uniquely different design as well. Matt McPherson is the president and owner of *Mathews Inc.* and it is his design that has scored so big in the archery world. But this inventor's engineering skills go beyond archery. Matt has developed a very clever sleeping system that replaces the standard sleeping bag. You won't freeze out in this baby, nor overheat as comfort was in mind at both ends of the thermometer. Additionally, his love for music has led him to manufacture custom built guitars and you'll find a number of big name musicians are pickin' and grinnin' on the strings of a *McPherson* guitar. Fishing has also taken a place at *Mathews Inc.* as custom built fly rods are produced at the Sparta, Wisconsin factory as well.

Fishing has been an outdoor activity Matt has been hooked on from his youth. But not all goes well when it comes to his angling adventures. Once while out with his father-in-law, Matt decided to show off his angling skills to impress his fishing partner. It was in the year of 1983 on a beautifully sunny, but very windy day on Millie Lacs Lake in Minnesota. The wind was making the water very rough which Matt can use as ammunition in his defense, but only slightly. Perhaps he was thrown off balance by the wave action at just the wrong time. We'll let you be the judge . Just remember, "Pride Cometh Before A Fall." The pair were fishing with live bait, minnows to be exact, and Matt had just hooked on a fresh fish. Preparing to launch his rig into the deep, he gave it all he was worth and it was an awesome cast. However, the failure to remove the bait fish's slime from his hands became a critical error, as the rod rocketed out of his grasp. It followed the minnow like a lost puppy as both dived below the water's surface. Matt remembers, "Panic went across my face and my father-in-law looks at me like, 'What's the matter with you!' I cried out, 'Throw out the anchor! Throw out the buoy, so we can mark the spot to see if we've drifted much!' "

With another fishing rod and a big Daredevil Spoon tied on, he dragged the bottom for ten to fifteen minutes. Finally hooking on the rod's line they were able to pull the tackle aboard.

Now Matt McPherson may have let pride get in his way on the fishing trip, but he didn't let pride defeat him when related to life eternal. You can also find a way around pride and have the peace that passes all understanding. To learn more, call, e-mail or write to God's Great Outdoors for the free booklet entitled, "More Than Winning & Losing," by Hank Parker. We'll also mail you Jim Grassi's "The Ultimate Fishing Challenge," too.

HERE'S A:
"MY BIGGEST HUNTING BLUNDER" FROM
"God's Great Outdoors"
#027

The designer of **PhotoStalk**, *Camouflage Systems*, Doug Prather has had a time when not being spotted by game animals or other hunters was the last thing in the world he wanted. You see, when you're lost in the wilderness one would wish the camo clothing they're wearing could suddenly be transformed to a flashy, bright neon lite outfit that could be seen from many miles away.

The event happened on a caribou hunt in Alaska where Doug was accompanied by his pastor and good friend Tony Cooper. The two had made several trips packing out a 600-lb. caribou that had been harvested. One more trip would finish the job at hand, so the pair decided to hunt their way back with the last of the downed animal. On this trip, they would be traveling solo and the men were given map quadrants to travel to and from their intended destinations. The problem was the quadrants were given to them off of a GPS. Doug and Tony only had conventional compasses and their location in Alaska was 15 degrees off magnetic north which was not taken into account. The sportsmen were reading the compass wrong, the result was being lost in the wilds of Alaska. As the day wore on the hunters realized they would be spending the night away from base camp. No one would be missing them or searching for them that night as the rest of the hunting party had flown off somewhere. Doug says, "The worst feeling in the world is being lost and knowing no one is looking for you."

The prospect of a very long night loomed before the men, they stopped to pray. Doug remembers, "We prayed as lost men would be expected to pray - earnestly!" In a few minutes after praying, as they continued the journey, a shed caribou antler was spotted which they thought they recognized from a previous trip through the area. Even though it was not the antler they had seen, nor were they in the same spot, it turned them left. Still lost, they ended the day's trek by a lake's head waters. As darkness settled around them, they thought they could hear distant voices, firing their rifles, the others they heard, wherever they were, responding in like manner. So, the men made camp with the provisions they had. Morning dawned with a heavy fog and Doug asked God, "Lord what do we do?" They were prepared to fire signal flares, but that would be useless. When the fog lifted they could see a float plane and were viewing the only humans of the area within fifty square miles. The fellow also turned out to be someone Doug knew and he flew them to their base camp. It turned out that they were only 1 ½ miles from their camp, going the wrong way. Doug Prather is convinced it was no accident and God had intervened. When he showed them the antler shed and started them left toward the only lake that had a plane or humans on it for fifty square miles. It should be noted that the two were lightly clothed and the night they stayed out was very low winds for the area, with temperatures in the low forties. The next night winds were 50-60 miles per hour and it rained two inches. One more night and the two would have most likely died of hypothermia.

Doug Prather was given a way to be rescued from the lost condition of the Alaskan wilderness, but may become lost again someday. However, he will never be lost eternally, as he's asked Jesus Christ to be Lord and Savior. Why not contact us here at God's Great Outdoors and we will send you a free booklet on the subject by Charlie Alsheimer called, "The Ultimate Hunt." You will also receive "The Greatest Hunt of All," by Dwight Schuh.

"Oops?"
#027

After fifteen years of burning welding rod and spinning a wrench on car haulers, "parking lots," as we called them, my job was downsized and relocated. My wife Cyndi and I felt God's hand in this as the radio program's work was more than a full-time job, and we had prayed for God to help me go full-time, and I lacked the faith to just up and quit. I was offered the chance to relocate to the new facility, plus four additional locations, but we decided to place our needs in God's hands at that point in our journey. I must say here, the Lord has met every need we have ever had, sometimes before we ever knew we had a need or thought to ask Him.

A year and a half later, one afternoon I received a call asking if I wanted to take a position at a major car hauler terminal. Still on the inactive seniority list, the company was required to call me, but I declined. Three weeks later I received a registered letter informing me I had ten days to show-up at the company's small operations office set-up at the auto manufacturing factory yard to fill out some papers. I had worked with over thirty mechanics there, now only half were still active with the company at some location. So, as I waited in the office to sign the form, I didn't think I would see any of my old work mates. Suddenly, there stood a fellow mechanic who also had refused the new location and received a letter. We exchanged greetings and talked a bit. Then, a supervisor we had worked with stepped in and soon he was asking a number of questions about the radio program, all the places I had traveled to and about the well-known outdoorsmen I was interviewing for God's Great Outdoors. I was actually to leave for Alaska the next day to speak at several churches and fill-in at a radio station for a number of weeks. I shared about the past year's trips and how I had interviewed Ron Lindner and Bill Dance plus some other outdoorsmen who are seen on television.

God had really opened some doors, we talked about that and the guys I used to work with there. After doing the required paperwork, the other mechanic had to leave, he shook my hand and wished me good luck, I said, "Thanks." Later, as I drove down the road, I thought about that. I don't believe in luck and I could have said so and preached a sermon to him about it. Yet, I marveled at God and how of all the ex-employees he could have sent there at that time, he was the one. First, he was one of the fishermen in the shop and watched *In-Fisherman* and other fishing TV shows. He had heard all God was doing in my life. Second, I had talked to him time and again about the Gospel, he knew the truth. Last, once I had lost my temper with him and we had gotten into a shouting match. I apologized, but our relationship had suffered since. His hand offered to me was taken as a friendly gesture, that was great.

Nothing happens by accident and as I said, I marveled, and still do, that he was there at that time. God is in control, if someone loves you enough to share God's truth about His Son Jesus and His death on the cross, it is no accident. Why not choose to accept that love from your friend and the living Savior this very day.

Revelation 3:20
"Here I am! I stand at the door and knock. If anyone hears my voice and opens the door, I will come in and eat with him, and he with me."

Isaiah 1:18
"'Come now, let us reason together', says the Lord. 'Though your sins are like scarlet, they shall be white as snow; though they are red as crimson, they shall be like wool.'"

Day Twenty-eight
HERE'S A: "ONE THAT GOT AWAY"
FISHING STORY FROM
"God's Great Outdoors"
#001

When it comes to losing in the area of fishing, the host of God's Great Outdoors, Gerry Caillouet, always strikes out big when he tries to hook into salmon or trout. But that's only when he's fishing with his brother-in-law, Joe Bakanovic.(back-a-no-vic) "It's like I'm jinxed anytime I fish with my brother-in-law Joe. He always out does me," says Gerry. But trout and salmon fishing seems to be a total washout if his brother-in-law is on the fishing excursion.

When fishing river banks for trout, Joe will be hauling in fish left and right and all Gerry is able to land are creek chubs. "Joe will be filling a stringer of trout as I play catch and release with the river's chubbies," laments Gerry. "But the worst times fishing with Joe is for salmon on the Great Lakes," Gerry remembers. "I can think of at least two times when everyone in the boat was catching salmon but me. We all used the same tackle and lures, but I came home empty handed each trip. The few fish I did hook, I lost! In fact, one of those times Joe even caught a beautiful steelhead that topped off his ice chest full of salmon." Gerry says this was like rubbing salt in his wound. And did his brother-in-law feel sorry for Gerry? "Not on your life,", reflects Gerry. "Joe just loved it!"

The host of God's Great Outdoors might lose out when fishing with his brother-in-law Joe, but there's one place Gerry is certainly a winner, and that is when it comes to his eternal salvation. You also can be a part of God's ultimate fishing creel and thus be assured of winning out for all eternity.

For a free booklet on the subject by Hank Parker, called "More Than Winning and Losing," contact God's Great Outdoors by mail, phone, or e-mail. You'll also receive a free copy of "The Ultimate Fishing Challenge," by Jim Grassi.

HERE'S A:
"MY BIGGEST HUNTING BLUNDER" FROM
"God's Great Outdoors"
#029

One of the most musically gifted men our host Gerry Caillouet knows is Ted Wilson. Ted can perform on just about every musical instrument in existence. He can also carry a tune vocally and has composed a number of songs and instrumental works. The fact is, some of Ted's pieces are heard right here on God's Great Outdoors. The theme of the program, the background music behind the **Wheel Power** *Christian Cyclists* spots, and *Let's Go Fishing Ministries* are some examples of his God given talent.

These days, Ted is the pastor of the praise & worship and adult ministries of Glenwood Community Church in Vancouver, Washington. But the view from the church has quite a pull on the outdoorsman side of this "man of the cloth." From the church building one can see three mountains. Mount St. Helen's, Silver Star and Mount Hood all looming in the distance, and in the forests below each of these peaks, roam elk, turkey, and black tail deer. So, if it's not the scenery itself Ted hears calling, it's the critters he looks forward to pursuing and that's where Ted's blunder took place. But it wasn't the wild game that made this woodsman whimper. The biggest pain to this Northwesterner's brain happened at the end of an elk hunt. As the weary and elkless sportsman returned to his vehicle, he laid his homemade recurve bow down to open the door and load his gear. However, when Ted got home and pulled out his stuff, the bow was missing. The bone weariness he'd been feeling was replaced with the energy that can accompany panic. However, the drive back found the bow had vanished and the panic was swallowed by the "you turkey" syndrome.

Which reminded Ted of a time years before when while hunting turkey in western Illinois, a big "Old Gobbler" had some foolery with him as the...well you know, he felt like a bit of a turkey himself. He'd been driving to chat with the farmer who'd given him permission to hunt, when he spied the tom in the middle of an alfalfa field. He parked his car out of sight and crawled to where he thought the Thanksgiving dinner should be, but .... it wasn't? Instead an old car tire was sticking slightly up out of the field, but there was no turkey. Only 20 feet away, the tire, really the turkey mind you, developed a turkey's head. Now Ted had his gun pointed right at the bird and a 3 to 4 minute stare down ensued. Ted decided he was going to shoot, when the bird blasted off, nothing happened as Ted squeezed the trigger. He'd never released the shotgun's safety. By the time he recovered and shot, all he had to take home was a couple of tail feathers.

Ted Wilson has felt like a turkey a time or two, but not when it comes to his position for eternity. He didn't get fooled here, as he's placed his trust in Jesus Christ and His shed blood which covers all sins! You can stop being a turkey too. To learn more, call, write, or e-mail us here at God's Great Outdoors and we'll send you a free booklet called, "The Ultimate Hunt," by Charlie Alsheimer. You'll also receive Dwight Schuh's, "The Greatest Hunt of All".

"What Goes Up, Must Come Down"
#028

"You've got to be sincere," yes it was the title of one of the songs sung by the character, Conrad Birdie in the movie, *Bye Bye Birdie*. But that is not where we are going. No, this is the thought of many people who look at religion and how they approach it. Understand, Jesus himself spoke against religion and the religious leaders of the day. He was inviting those who had an ear to hear, to a personal relationship with Him and the Father in Heaven. He called everyone no matter how bad they were, to this relationship. His claims were of one with authority, never before had the people heard someone speak like Jesus Christ. And, never has anyone spoken like Him since, nor will they, as He is the Creator God, in the flesh.

Sincerity in a belief doesn't mean it is the way to eternal life. For example, suppose a group of people listening to a man who speaks on the religion of *No Gravity* can be convinced by his clever argument that gravity is only in the mind. He claims if you let go of those beliefs you will not be effected by the fake force science has invented and the world was duped into accepting from early childhood. Preached long enough, the man may become a leader and gain many followers. With time the group wanting to show other people the truth and reveal the lie decides to act. As one body they ascend a forty story building and prepare to free the masses from their restrictive blinders. Together they step off, then suddenly and rapidly, the reality of gravity hits them right between the eyes. Why? Because being sincere wouldn't nullify physical laws. Reality and truth do exist and you can find them if you ask God to direct you to them. He will honor that prayer! Understand this, just as physical laws exist, there are also spiritual laws that cannot be laid aside simply because we desire it to be another way.

Did you know that law enforcement officials when learning how to recognize counterfeit money never see the fakes? They are given real tinder to examine and become intimately familiar with. When done, they know what the genuine thing looks like and bogus bills are easy to spot. We have the real thing, the Bible, and anyone who says you can't understand it on your own and must have someone teach you the truth may be sincere, but they are wrong. The Bible is the spoken word of God in written form. When Jesus was on the earth He spoke directly to the people and when you read the Bible, the same thing still happens.

John 14:6
"Jesus answered, 'I am the way and the truth and the life. No one comes to the Father except through me.'"

John 5:24
"I tell you the truth, whoever hears my word and believes him who sent me has eternal life and will not be condemned; he has crossed over from death to life."

Day Twenty-nine
HERE'S A: "ONE THAT GOT AWAY"
FISHING STORY FROM
"God's Great Outdoors"
#031

Having an enjoyment of the outdoors and making a living at doing that activity too, is a dream many share. Well, two men who love to fish and canoe decided to take a leap of faith and begin building and selling their idea of the perfect fishing, functional and fun, water craft on the water. Bill Plantan and Dave Frink are joint owners of *River Ridge Custom Canoes* out of Rochester, Minnesota. And while things in the boat business are doing quite well, the fishing adventures sometimes sour. Here's one of Bill Plantan's maritime mistakes.

When his daughter Sarah, was going into the ninth grade, she joined her dad on a float trip down the Red Cedar in Wisconsin. When they reached the mouth where the Red Cedar empties into the Chippawa River, the two beached for the night. The sun was setting on that warm 85 degree mosquito filled evening, as they crawled into the tent. About three that morning, Bill's daughter awoke to answer nature's call. Sarah discovered that their canoe was gone and informed Bill. "What!" was Bill's excited and now wide awake response. Bill discovered that over the night, the dam up river let water out and the river level had risen enough to catch the canoe. The pair was deep in wilderness, ten miles from the nearest road. They were in the middle of nowhere. Bill told Sarah, "Honey, let's just wait. First sign of daylight at four thirty we'll go out and maybe it's along the shore. But right now, it's too dark and I can't see anything." So they returned to the tent to try and sleep.

At first light Bill stepped out and without his contacts, he thought that he could see something down the river that was bright yellow. Bill said, "I can see something." Then Sarah exclaimed, "Dad! I think the canoe is down there!" The water craft had drifted down until both lures on the fishing rods left inside, had caught a tangle of branches above the water. Problem was, the canoe was directly above a huge jam of trees right down stream from it's fixed position. Bill told Sarah, "Honey, no problem, I'll just walk along shore down there, free the canoe up and bring it back up here." They were both ecstatic that their transportation could be returned. However, upon his arrival to Bill's surprise, the minute he went in the water it was over his head. Dog paddling in the swift flow, he struggled to stay lined up with the canoe and not be carried away by the main current. On the way down, his little finger hit a log and was impaled by a long since forgotten Bomber fishing plug. Bill had to break off the end of the log as he couldn't free himself. Swimming with the piece of log, he made it to the boat which was barely being held by the lures in the tangle of overhead branches.

"First thing I did, thank the Lord, I had a pair of pliers in the bottom of the canoe. I took the pliers and was able to jerk the hook off of my hand." With the lure off, Bill surveyed the situation and decided to use the trolling motor to shoot him into the main current and away from the log jam. So, all in one operation while hanging onto the side of the canoe, he started the motor, cut the two fishing lines and steered his way into the flow and a safe place to beach, get inside and return to Sarah.

Bill Plantan has since learned to always anchor his canoe when he rests for the night. Bill blew it on that trip, but not on the journey through life, as he has anchored his future in Christ Jesus. To learn how you can too, contact us here at God's Great Outdoors and ask for your free copy of Hank Parker's "More Than Winning & Losing". We also will send "The Ultimate Fishing Challenge" by Jim Grassi.

HERE'S A:
"MY BIGGEST HUNTING BLUNDER" FROM
"God's Great Outdoors"
#030

Every year, more and more people travel to Africa to hunt the amazing variety of game animals that inhabit the Dark Continent. You see, despite the misinformation sometimes given by the media, wildlife populations are increasing everywhere regulated sports hunting is permitted. One case in point is elephants, where ironically, the countries that allow limited elephant hunts are the same locations the elephants' numbers are growing. Why? This is because all the people are benefitting, from the outfitter to the natives who get the meat! For this reason, poaching has been dramatically reduced, as everyone looks to lose when an elephant is shot just for it's ivory tusks. Krause, nicknamed "Buks," and Elna Botha own and operate *Bateleur Safaris* in the Republic of South Africa. Now, "Buks" doesn't take his clients out after the dangerous game known as the "Big Five," which includes the elephant. However, if you hunt with this professional hunter, there is no shortage of opportunities you may encounter. Sixteen different species of antelope plus Wart Hogs and Bush Pigs can be harvested while under "Buks'" watchful care and guidance.

Problem is, there are times when clients don't follow the directions "Buks" has given them; even after they agree with him on what he has said. You might say their excitement runs away with them. For example, one fellow from Alaska was hunting for a trophy Duiker. This small antelope spends it's days in the grassy and tree laden areas of the lands "Buks" guides his clients on. When two animals appear to the men on an unusually rainy day, "Buks" whispered, "Don't shoot." The eager client answered, "Ok." and shot anyway. Instead of a Duiker, he'd bagged a young Impala! But the clients aren't the only ones who react on impulse.

"A young hunter from California was with me in the bush and we were looking for kudu the third day in a row," remembers "Buks." "I see the one about seventy yards away, giving us a full broadside shot and I tell him to take it. The .338 roars and I hear the shot hitting hard, but kudu runs and we follow with our eyes till he disappears in the thick stuff." "Buks" continues, "After waiting the normal few minutes for it to go down, we walk to the place where it stood hoping to pick up a blood trail and finding it. Half way there it appears right where it disappeared earlier and I tell my client to hit it again right in the chest and again, I hear the 250 grainer slamming hard. We walk straight to where it was and find it stone dead. Happy hunter, lots of pictures and we bring the truck in to load. Something starts bothering me, and after breakfast I ask my skinner to make sure where the second shot had hit and he confirms that there is only one shot on the animal. I get this bad feeling and we go back to where the second shot was fired, but find a few tracks and no blood. A couple of days later, the landowner phoned me and confirmed my fears. He picked up the other (bigger) kudu about five-hundred yards further. The shot was a little far back and the animal ran for a while .... while the first one was dead already and laying right where the second one came out of the bush....so we keep learning! Who would have thought that another kudu will stand around while the shot rang and we were around talking to each other!!!"

Now Krause "Buks" Botha might have chosen wrongly on the day a kudu reappeared, which later in retrospect, brought fear to his mind, but that choice was not going to effect him for eternity. No, the choice that removes all fear was made by "Buks" when he asked Jesus Christ to be Lord and Savior. You can have all worry about this removed too. To learn more, call, write, or e-mail us here at God's Great Outdoors and we will send a free copy of "The Ultimate Hunt," by Charlie Alsheimer. You'll also get a copy of Dwight Schuh's, "The Greatest Hunt of All".

"Biting The Hand That Feeds You"
#029

I had spoken at a game dinner near Cleveland, Ohio when I heard an amazing story of the power of God and how His message of love can cross every language barrier. My wife Cyndi and I were chatting with some of those who had attended the event after it ended. A husband was sharing with us how his wife had worked for many years before their marriage with a native tribe in a remote back country location. Her job was to translate the Bible into this tribe's own tongue. All went well until she tried to convert John 6:26, *"I am the bread of life."* This people group had no word for bread, they had never seen bread and had no idea what bread was. So, this dear Christian sister inspired with godly wisdom wrote down "I am the sweet potato of life." It created the very word picture they needed as the sweet potato was their daily sustenance. The result? People's lives were transformed by the power of the Living God, as they received Jesus Christ as Savior.

I had been totally delighted by the story of this missionary's work. Yet, at the same time saddened too. Why? Because there are Christians who would be angered by this action of putting God's word into a different translation other than the King James Version. The notion that the King James translation is the only translation that "God has approved" is sadly not just argued between Christians behind closed doors. No, it is carried into the workplace at break rooms, and other public arenas. Christian books, radio, and now the Internet are creating a spectacle for those who need the real truth and just happen to be caught in the middle of these debates as they take place.

The point is not being addressed here to reveal a better translation today, as always the best sources are the original Hebrew, Greek, and Aramaic texts. No, the sad thing is, Christians arguing their points in front of non-believers. Then when the dust clears the combatants try to win these same people to Christ's love. How this must hurt God! It would serve the mission so much better if those wishing to discuss doctrinal differences were to gather in private. Christians don't need to make themselves or Jesus Christ who we claim changes our lives look bad. The world will work to do that for us, rest assured.

If you've been turned off to the message of God's love because of Christians' arguments over Bible versions, baptism, denominations, style of music used in church, "once saved, always saved," the tribulation sequence, or other such things, remember we are still like you, humans who fail our Lord God. Don't let that be a reason for rejecting God and spending eternity separated from the Lord and Savior, Jesus Christ.

Ephesians 4:29-32
"Do not let any unwholesome talk come out of your mouths, but only what is helpful for building others up according to their needs, that it may benefit those who listen. And do not grieve the Holy Spirit of God, with whom you were sealed for the day of redemption. Get rid of all bitterness, rage and anger, brawling and slander, along with every form of malice. Be kind and compassionate to one another, forgiving each other, just as in Christ God forgave you."

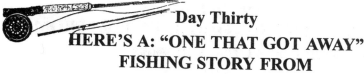

Day Thirty
HERE'S A: "ONE THAT GOT AWAY"
FISHING STORY FROM
"God's Great Outdoors"
#032

Now diehard fisherman will go out no matter what. Like the postman on his appointed rounds, when the local fishing forecast say they're biting, the hardcore angler is out there.

Ken Conlee, the President of the *Fellowship of Christian Angler Society*, also known as *FOCAS*, is one of those tough guys. Ken remembers that day, a cold, cloudy, misty February day some years back. He'd been out most of the day, on Lake Weatherford, which is located in the Lone Star state of Texas. Having finished fishing for the day, Ken had returned to the marina. As he steered his bass boat into one of the slips to tie up, he noticed some commotion going on.

Now the *FOCAS* President had been fishing minnows for crappie. But with the type of activity he was seeing he figured it had to be more than just a good haul of crappie. Two good old boys a couple of slips over in an old aluminum John boat were grinning from ear to ear. So, Ken after tying up his craft, walked over. These guys had been fishing for crappie too, but one of them had hooked into a huge largemouth bass. The fish was big enough to possibly be a new lake record. So, Ken headed back to his boat to get his camera. Trouble was, he forgot there were a couple of boat slips between the good old boy's vessel and his. The next thing Ken knew, he was up to his ears in 20-feet of cold water with an audience looking on! The thirty-four degree air temperature didn't warm his spirits either.

Now that was off camera. Once while filming a segment for Jimmy Houston's fishing show, Ken went overboard as it was being caught on the video camera. Falling head first into an icy cold lake in late winter, Ken remembers the incredible temperature shock. It momentarily caused him to be unable to catch his breath. All the while Jimmy Houston and two others from the crew roared with laughter and all on video to review when warm and dry.

When God reviews your life will you be found a winner with Jesus like Ken Conlee? Or will you lose with Satan and his followers? Now is the day of salvation. To learn more, contact us here at God's Great Outdoors by mail, phone, or e-mail for a free booklet by Hank Parker called, "More Than Winning and Losing," and you will also get "The Ultimate Fishing Challenge," by Jim Grassi.

HERE'S A:
"MY BIGGEST HUNTING BLUNDER" FROM
"God's Great Outdoors"
#031

Almost two decades ago, Dave Tripiciano (Trip-a-Chon-o) of *"My Father's World" Video Ministries* started having some of God's creatures looking up to him. Which is not a good thing if it is a deer and you are bowhunting them. Dave recalls, "I put a bottle of deer lure on a stump right under my tree stand and commenced climbing up into my treestand. I'm pulling my bow up and I look down and here's a buck sniffing the bottle. My bow is swinging back and forth almost in his face. And he looks up and looks at the bow and then looks right up at me." The then much wiser deer took off through the early October afternoon's crisp fall woodland.

Do the years and gained experience now count in this New York hunter's favor? Well not always. On a recent hunt, Dave was hoping to fill the freezer with venison one fall evening. He was in his treestand which he had wedged in among three Y-shaped branches of a fairly small tree. Dave reflects about the stands placement, "It was no really big heavy trunk, it was "jerry rigged" - strapped and bungeed-in. It was safe, but it would move a little when you put your weight on it the wrong way." One of the first times Dave was in the stand, he spotted a buck as it turned and came right to him. Dave was about to get his "dream shot," when - well, as he relocated his feet a little bit, shifting his weight and torqueing his body into the perfect position to draw his bow, the treestand moved amid his pre-shot preparation. The unexpected movement of his stand induced a wave of panic and instinctively Dave reached out to grab one of the tree's branches. As he did, he dropped his bow string release which fell right past the approaching buck's nose. The deer looked down at the release, then up at Dave above him and then it was "Hasta La Vista Baby."

Dave Tripiciano may have blown it a time or two where hunting is concerned, but in the hunt for eternal life Dave has hit the mark dead center with his Creator, Jesus Christ. You too can have life everlasting where there will be no more tears, pain or death. To learn more write, e-mail, or phone us here at God's Great Outdoors to receive a booklet on the subject by Charlie Alsheimer called, "The Ultimate Hunt." We will also send you "The Greatest Hunt of All," by Dwight Schuh.

"The Straw That Broke The Camel's Back"
#030

The Viet Nam war was heating up when Davey Roever received his draft notice. Now he could have gotten a deferment because he was a college student who was studying for the ministry, yet Davey wondered why he shouldn't go if others were going. Soon he was kissing his new bride good-by and traveling to his place in a U.S. Navy river boat in the heat of battle. One day during a fire fight a phosphorus hand grenade exploded in his hand burning off half of his face plus multiple other injuries.

T.R. Michels is an outdoor writer, speaker, outfitter, and professional guide. But life hasn't always been so exciting as the arena he now works in. In 1977, life's issues topped off and started to overflow. When his girlfriend left him, he became depressed and even though he was a Christian who knew God's love, he attempted suicide by placing a 12-gauge shot gun in his mouth. Despite this mistake, with one-third of his face blown away, Michels survived the ordeal and the multiple surgeries performed for the next ten years.

These men have two things in common. One, they are Believers in the Lord Jesus Christ and God has a plan to use them in carrying out *The Great Commission*. Davey Roever is an evangelist who reaches teens and adults with the love of Jesus Christ all over the world. T.R. Michels shares the Gospel with unsaved outdoorsmen and other groups anywhere he is given the chance. Second, neither of these men were expected to live, but God is always in control even when it appears everything is out of control.

Having such scars or birth defects can bring stares and mean remarks from others that can hurt very much emotionally. With time scars can develop inside that are far worse and turn into bitterness. Do you have an anger burning down inside of you? Perhaps someone hurt you in other ways. A parent dies or leaves home never to return, the color of your skin or your nationality, physical and sexual abuse; all can be areas where others can strike at us and all these will scar us too. We can be wronged in so many ways. If something is being brought to your mind as you read this, it is God's Holy Spirit trying to draw out whatever it is in your life that has left scar tissue on your heart. Even if it was a Christian who wronged you and for this reason you want nothing to do with their God, the Spirit is saying to let it go. He can turn the pain and tragedy of life into so many wonderful things! Simply come to Jesus, put down your weapons of war and rebellion, and you will see what I mean.

Matthew 11:28
"Come to me, all you who are weary and burdened, and I will give you rest."

John 8:36
"So if the Son sets you free, you will be free indeed."

Day Thirty-one
HERE'S A: "ONE THAT GOT AWAY"
FISHING STORY FROM
"God's Great Outdoors"

Written By Bill Snodgrass And Edited For Radio Broadcast By Gerry Caillouet
#033

Bill Snodgrass has quite a few years of hunting and fishing under his belt. As the owner of *Bill Snodgrass' Big Game Hunts*, Bill puts all that knowledge to use. Yet, some of the know-how Bill has comes from past mistakes both hunting and fishing. Bill begins reflecting on one of his early boo-boo's. "When I was younger, much younger, we would take our children on vacation to Canada. I was somewhat new to fishing and laid into a big Walleye. I estimate him to have been between six to seven pounds. I just about had him to the boat and the knot holding the plug came loose. I watched my trophy swim away, all because I had not taken time to prepare the proper knot".

Bill always tries to relate life's experiences into a spiritual application through God's holy word in the Bible. He went on to say, "You know, we as Christians must take time to prepare our daily walk and witness. Are you using the proper knot throughout life, from God's word?"

Another time Bill was Muskie fishing and saw a big Muskie roll as they fished around a big weed bed on the edge of the lake. Now, Muskie are a prize catch stocked on many lakes across the nation. They are much larger than their cousins, the Pike. Large Muskie have been known to consume ducks and muskrats.

Bill cast to this monster of the weed bed. The fish hit Bill's plug with a great forceful strike and he set the hook. The fight was on and eventually the crew of the small boat was able to bring the fish on board. At forty-eight inches long and weighing twenty-six pounds, it was a real trophy. Bill was excited, a little too excited and the little boy inside every grown man escaped. Bill began to jump up and down in the small boat and water started to run in over the sides of the boat. Thankfully, Bill stopped before the crew was in real peril.

There is another place all of us are in real peril, and that's trying to cross from life to death without making peace with God through Jesus Christ. To find out how to safely make the passage, we have a free booklet on the subject by Hank Parker called, "More Than Winning and Losing." Contact us here at God's Great Outdoors by mail, phone, or e-mail and we'll send both Hank Parker's booklet and "The Ultimate Fishing Challenge," by Jim Grassi.

HERE'S A:
"MY BIGGEST HUNTING BLUNDER" FROM
"God's Great Outdoors"
#032

Since 1970 Louie and Nancy Horwath, (hor-wuth) have provided opportunities for bear and moose hunters and fishermen at their Blind River Ontario location, called *Louie's Outpost*. And with all these people coming and going, you can be sure everything doesn't always go as planned. Ten years ago, Louie was motoring across the lake to pick-up one of his fall bear hunters who was babysitting an excellent bait location. With the sun setting, Louie neared the shore, but something in the water caught his eye. Suddenly, his mind identified the hunter, chest-deep in the lake's water, holding his rifle over his head. Louie says, "I couldn't imagine what had happened. Well, early in the evening he had shot at a bear and missed it. The bear on exiting, ran by the hunter at five feet. He panicked and went out in the lake and had been there a couple of hours waiting for me to come and pick him up. He was very chilled, everything on his body was chattering."

Now that story is a bit humorous, but not every mishap Louie has had is. When they were first getting the business started, a very serious incident occurred. Louie was watching a hunter go up a tree with a self-climbing treestand. The spring bear hunter suddenly flipped over backwards. The early self-climbing stands had leather straps on the base. With his feet stuck in the leather straps, the hunter was hanging upside down sixteen feet above the ground and couldn't do anything. In his panicked state, Louie's first attempt to climb the tree was unsuccessful. He remembers, "I tried pushing him up with a log I dragged out of the bush and he couldn't stand the pain of any of that. And after five or six minutes he seemed to be going into shock. So I managed to climb the tree and cut one strap and he was swinging, dangling by one leg. When I cut the other strap, the treestand swung sideways and hit me in the side of the head."

When Louie came to, he was crawling around on the ground and the hunter lay at the tree's base moaning and groaning. Both went to the hospital, the hunter spending his remaining week of hunting there, with ten more months on crutches at home.

Now Louie Horwath has experienced accidents firsthand, but it was no accident when he asked Jesus Christ to be his Lord and Savior. You also can receive everlasting life through Jesus. To learn more, contact us here at God's Great Outdoors by phone, mail, or e-mail and ask for Charlie Alsheimer's booklet titled, "The Ultimate Hunt." We will also send "The Greatest Hunt of All," by Dwight Schuh.

"Mirror, Mirror On The Wall"
#031

In 1998 God's Great Outdoors had a booth at the *National Religious Broadcaster's Convention and Expo* in Washington, D.C. We were there with several of the leaders of outdoor ministries who the radio program works with. The reason for being there was to talk to station managers and hopefully see the program added to more stations across the country. Twice while in the booth something interesting happened. First, a businessman in sales attending the event tried his pitch on us about his business' services. But, as we talked I sensed this man's need for Christ. When he finished the informative time, I asked if I might ask a question about his spiritual life. With a positive reply, I asked, "If you were to die this minute are you certain beyond a shadow of a doubt that you would be ushered into the presence of God?" He wasn't, and several of us proceeded to present the Gospel, which we learned he was not a stranger to and in the end just wasn't ready to receive.

Later, a writer for a very well-known national magazine stepped into the booth and started picking up one of everything we had to give away. Soon we discovered this woman wrote the religious section and she too needed Christ! However, her reaction to our inquiries was to flat-out stop us by stating, "I'll read what you've given me!" Thinking about these two people I wondered, with all the Christian media present, several thousand, had anyone else shared God's love with these two people? Or in such an environment was everyone assuming everyone else to be a Believer in Christ? I cannot answer for them, but if this is the first time you've ever heard about God the Father's love, His Son Jesus who died for you and the Holy Spirit who is moving on your heart in an effort to have you allow Jesus Christ to save you from your sins, I'm sorry. We Christians are human and will fail, but God will never fail you. When you begin a personal relationship with Him you will understand what I am saying.

If you've heard all this before and you are still lost in your sins, what is holding you back? I've seen peer pressure effect adults, keeping them from God's saving grace. The love of money has pulled many down to the pits of Hell. With money comes power, but it ends with death. Pride is hated by God, perhaps it is the biggest reason people will spend eternity in the Lake of Fire. In reality, your position on this earth compares to one grain of sand on a vast beach stretching in both directions as far as the eye can see! Up close in a mirror you may appear impressive, but scattered among the other specks of sand who could pick you out? Yet despite your insignificance Jesus Christ suffered an excruciating death and He did it for you. He is calling all who will, to receive Him to be their Lord and Savior. Please come now, this may be the last chance you will have.

Romans 3:10-12
"As it is written: 'There is no one righteous, not even one; there is no one who understands, no one who seeks God. All have turned away, they have together become worthless; there is no one who does good, not even one.'"

Hebrews 9:27,28
"Just as man is destined to die once, and after that to face judgment, so Christ was sacrificed once to take away the sins of many people; and he will appear a second time, not to bear sin, but to bring salvation to those who are waiting for him."

The Trails End

HERE'S A: "ONE THAT GOT AWAY" FISHING STORY FROM
"God's Great Outdoors"
#030

As an outdoor writer, he's been able to fish all over the world. But Stan Fagerstrom's (fag-er-strom) claim to fame is his incredible casting ability. With over fifty years of trick casting under his belt he's known as the "Master Caster," but Stan says, "Sometimes I'm not as good as I think I am." Here's Stan Fagerstrom's fishing blunder.

For many years, Stan made it a practice to go before a sports show opened and warm up, honing his skills for an hour or more, just one cast after another at small targets and practice his trick casts. Well, one day at the *King Dome* in Seattle, Washington, before the International Sportsman Exposition opened, Stan was there early. All was quiet as he practiced casting at a paper coffee cup thirty feet away.

Stan remembers, "I'm casting with a casting rod and casting reel and I cast and WHAPP! right in the middle of that cup. I sensed someone walk up along side to my left, even though the show isn't open yet. I didn't pay attention and cast again, WHAPP! right in the cup. A voice says, 'My goodness! Can you do that every time?' I answered, 'You bet!' Which was my first mistake. The fellow said, 'Let's see you do it again!' So I cast and WHAPP! right in the middle of the cup. Three in a row. The man asked me, 'Could you do that on television?' I said, 'Why not?' Which was my second mistake. The fella said, 'Listen, do it one more time.' SHEEE------SMACK! right in the middle of the cup! He said excitedly, 'Mr. Fagerstrom, I'm the host of *PM Magazine*, very popular here in Seattle. I'm going to be here tonight at the very opening of the show, we're going to do a live spot. That would be terrific to have you hit that cup out there, can you do it?' To which I smartly replied, 'No problem!' Which became mistake number three. 'Alright, have your gear and be ready by the entrance at about 7:25, we're on promptly at 7:30 and we're going to come on with you,' stated the TV host. Stan assured him he'd be there. As 7:20 arrived, the 'Master Caster' wandered over in that direction which was seeing quite a crowd gather as they tend to do with TV cameras present. Soon the producer was counting down saying '4-3-2-1' and the well-known host was on air live. 'Ladies and gentlemen, we have something that you've never seen before and might never see for a long time in the future. We have Stan Fagerstrom, this guy can hit a paper cup with a cast thirty feet away and he never misses!' The show's host went on and on as Stan stood watching the cup shrink to the size of a thimble. Finally, stepping back he let Stan do his thing. 'Show them how you can hit the cup!' Stan cast and missed! He was off at least three feet! Stan reflects, 'I wished there was a hole I could have slithered down through and gotten out of there; I would have, but there wasn't.' Reeling in and thank heavens with the next cast I got right in the middle of the cup!"

We all have put too much confidence in our abilities a time or two, but Stan Fagerstrom is wise enough to know his ability and effort will fall short of getting right with God, no matter how hard he tries. That's why he's trusted in Jesus Christ as his Savior, and you can too. For more information, contact God's Great Outdoors to receive a free copy of Hank Parker's "More Than Winning & Losing." You'll also receive "The Ultimate Fishing Challenge," by Jim Grassi.

HERE'S A:
"MY BIGGEST HUNTING BLUNDER" FROM
"God's Great Outdoors"
#028

In reflection of past hunting blunders, the President of *Buck Knives*, Chuck Buck, shared how he was almost seriously injured. Chuck was hunting with a couple of other men on Queen Charlotte Island, which is located 100 miles west of Vancouver, British Columbia.

This was a guided hunt for the coastal blacktail deer that inhabit the lush rain soaked forests of this Canadian Province. One of the men in the party happened to be an outdoor writer who was showing a different side than his readers might experience. The gentleman had failed to remember to pack along his binoculars which is critical in spotting the elusive blacktail bucks. So, he kept asking to borrow Chuck's, who needed them too. Also, the journalist would use his rifle's scope to scan for game. Chuck was fearful for other hunters who may be hunting where this unthinking hunter was pointing his firearm. Chuck shared with the man the hunting safety rules he was breaking, rules taught in every hunting safety course. But the incident that most frightened Chuck and the rest of the group happened in a split second. Chuck recalls, "We were walking a trail and I was walking in front of the other guy who was behind me. All of a sudden his rifle went off pointed almost at me. I could feel the air as the bullet went past my leg. It just scared us all, we jumped, probably every deer in the area jumped too."

It turned out this outdoor writer had a hair trigger on his rifle, never had it repaired and was not concerned enough to practice safe hunting techniques: but was that the worst incident in Chuck Buck's bag of outdoor related blunders? No, one event has burned a deeper scar in his conscious.

It happened in San Diego, California when Chuck was to receive an award from the "Alumni Eagle Association" of the *Boy Scouts of America*. *Buck Knives* gives all the young men who make Eagle Scout a new *Buck Knife* with their names engraved on the blade. The alumni was thanking *Buck Knives* for these gifts over the years. Now Chuck arrived late to the event which was underway. Noticing the speaker at the podium and the approximately 70 people in the room, he saw no empty seats. Then he spotted one at the head table. Chuck says, "I thought, 'Well they're going to honor me, maybe that's where I'm going to sit.' So, I went up and acted like I was doing what I thought I should do." Now the guy sitting next to him was a friend and leaned over and said, "Chuck, I think you're supposed to be sitting right over there," pointing to an empty chair in the audience.

Chuck adds, "There was a seat, sure enough, you can imagine my feelings of getting up in front of all of those guys and feeling bad that I was so presumptuous. That verse in the Bible about don't sit at the seat of honor, sit at the back then if the man of the house wants you there in the seat of honor, he will guide you up."

Chuck Buck could have lost his life on the blacktail trip, but he will still have a place of honor as he stands before God who judges every man, woman and child, not by what they have done or not done, but by what Jesus Christ did on the cross for us all. To learn more and receive a free booklet by Charlie Alsheimer called, "The Ultimate Hunt," contact us here at God's Great Outdoors, either by mail, phone, or e-mail and we will send one to you. You'll get "The Greatest Hunt of All," by Dwight Schuh.

The Longest Day?

On June 6th, 1944, American and Allied troops landed on the beaches of France and parachuted or landed by glider plane among the hedgerow country inland from the coastal assault. The greatest invasion force ever assembled began an attack we still marvel at to this day.

In the recent motion picture about the Normandy conflict, a glimpse of the sacrifice these men made for freedom is revealed. As the last battle scene ends in the movie *Saving Private Ryan*, the mortally wounded Captain Miller speaks to the young private from Iowa. His words relate to James Frances Ryan, that he should make the deaths of his men and himself count. The notion that the earning of a good life is received by this paratrooper is revealed years later as the veteran stands over the grave of the same fallen Army officer. After talking to the head-stone of the captain about his own efforts to try to live a good life, he stands. Then he turns to his wife asking what seem to be haunting questions to this old man. With great emotion he asks his wife if he has been living a life one would consider good. Before she can answer, James Ryan inquires more directly by asking his wife to tell him what manner of man he has been, was he one she'd call good? What struck me as I watched the movie's ending was not only the sadness of these heros we lost in this decisive battle of World War II. But that this man had to wonder and then ask if he was a man of value to others. One has to ask of Private Ryan's question, does just being called a good man count for anything in the end anyway? Will it have value in allowing you to spend eternity in the presence of God? And by what standard does one measure where good starts or where good ends?

Had the force's landing in Normandy been defeated by Hitler's troops, the results would have been devastating to the allies. Years of planning and preparation lay on the line, not to mention hundreds of thousands of lives. A defeat that day would have dealt a blow that would be difficult to recover from without much passage of time. The world's balance hung by a thread on the morning *Operation Overlord,* as it was code named, began. That is why it has been spoken of as the *Longest Day.* But as long as that day may have seemed to those waiting on news of the invasion and in the midst of the conflict, it was still only a twenty-four hour period. There is a longest day - eternity, for each of us, and it begins on the day we die. Two paths await those who crossover death's doorstep. One towards everlasting separation from God in the fires of Hell, the other in the presence of the Almighty where there is no more pain, tears, or suffering. Stepping before Jesus Christ who will judge us all is not a time to wonder, was I a good man, woman, or child. You must understand no one is good enough to stand before a Holy God, as we are all sinners and sin, any sin separates us from God. *"For the wages of sin is death, but the gift of God is eternal life in Christ*

114

Jesus our Lord" (Romans 6:23). But, God loved us so much He did not want any of us to join Satan and his demons in the Lake of Fire.

For me, a person who grew up in a church that taught works *might* get one to Heaven, one Bible passage clicked for me. It was in the book of Luke, the 23rd chapter starting with the 39th verse. You see here, a realization about the reality of the moment has taken place and has lead to a changed heart. In Matthew 27:44, we see both men being crucified with Jesus joining everyone else and making fun of Him and His situation. But the book of Luke records what transpires as the hours have passed. At this point one of the thieves has realized he is in the same position as Jesus and is about to die too. And he also understands now that Jesus is who he has said he is, the Messiah, God in the flesh, who has come to save the world from it's sins. So, when the other thief again asks Jesus to save himself and them too, his partner speaks out,

"One of the criminals who hung there hurled insults at him: 'Aren't you the Christ? Save yourself and us!' But the other criminal rebuked him. 'Don't you fear God, he said, 'since you are under the same sentence? We are punished justly, for we are getting what our deeds deserve. But this man has done nothing wrong." Then he said, "Jesus, remember me when you come into your kingdom." Jesus answered him, "I tell you the truth, today you will be with me in paradise." (Luke 23: 39-42) Here we see the man who defends Jesus, realizing he is a sinner, having sorrow for those sins and calling on the only one who can remove them by the power of the blood He was shedding. Then Jesus lets him know he will be welcomed into the presence of God that very day. No deeds to perform, no list of people who say he was a good man needed, simply by the blood poured out on the cross at Calvary. Salvation is a gift of God that comes by faith, not of anything we may accomplish. In other words, it is not what we do, but what Jesus Christ did for us. We simply need to accept this truth and receive His forgiveness by faith, it is that easy.

It is my sincere hope that you can say that if you died this moment you would be with Jesus Christ instantly and you believe this beyond a shadow of a doubt. But, if you cannot say this, will you as the thief on the cross, now pray this simple sinner's prayer. "Jesus I'm a sinner and I'm sorry for these sins in my life. I ask you to forgive me and come into my life and heart and become the Lord of my life. Direct my paths from this day forward and thank you for giving your life's blood for me, in Jesus' name I pray, Amen."

Now if you've prayed this prayer, we would be happy to know and would like to help you on your journey with Christ Jesus. And you can have the assurance you will spend life everlasting with the Lord. *"I tell you the truth, whoever hears my word and believes him who sent me has eternal life and will not be con-*

demned; he has crossed over from death to life." (John 5:24)

If, however, you still feel this is a bunch of nonsense I leave you with this thought. If I am wrong, when I die, I have lost nothing. But, If I am right and you die in your present condition, you've lost everything! The choice is yours to make, I pray you will choose wisely, for you will have begun, at the time of your death your *Longest Day!*

You've prayed the simple prayer, we have a booklet that we would like to send you, to help you on this journey with Jesus Christ.

It's called;

ANSWERS TO LIVE BY
By Edwin D. Roels
Published by; The Bible League
Contact us today:

God's Great Outdoors
8193 Emerick Road
West Milton, OH 45383
(937) 698-3656
Toll Free # 1-877-TALKGGO
E-Mail: ggoutdoors@aol.com

HERE'S A: "ONE THAT GOT AWAY" FISHING STORY FROM
"God's Great Outdoors"

Written By Dave Watson And Edited For Radio Broadcast By Gerry Caillouet

#019

TNN's, *Bushnell's Secrets of the Hunt,* is hosted and produced by Dave Watson. Dave remembers his biggest fishing foul-up. "Everyone knows my friend Jim, although everyone seems to call him by a different name. Some call him "Jimbo," others call him "Jim Bob" or even "Jimmy The Z." Then there's always the old reliable "Zumbo." Some people even add "mister" as a prefix, I guess out of respect. After all, he has worked very hard to become the Hunting Editor of *Outdoor Life* magazine and he has earned that respect. I agree, but I still call him Jim, he knows I respect him, even without the "mister." I might know him too well. I know his love of fishing is as great as his love of hunting. I also know he's always up for a practical joke, so I didn't fall for his praise of my first catch on the Wise River in Montana.

"That's a fine Brookie, Davey. They don't get much bigger than that," Jim said. "Yeah, right, he's barely six inches long, I'm not falling for that," I thought to myself. "You seem to have found a honey hole. I'll go down stream so I don't disturb you," Jim said as he fought the pine limbs that guarded the bank of the river. "That's another thing about Jim. He's a true gentleman with unquestionable ethics and stream side manners.

"I spent the next two hours throwing back more six inch Brook Trout that I could count. Brook Trout, just like all of God's creations are beautiful. A sublime mixture of rich tans, browns and greens that dart through the crystal clear waters of almost every river and stream in Montana. Upon my return to camp, Jim had the fire going and the smell of fish frying filled the mountain air, I hadn't realized how hungry I was! I peeked over into the pan as the hot oil bubbled around the trout. Most of them were three or four inches in length, with the whoppers coming near the six inch mark. Jim had been serious when he told me that Brookies don't get much bigger than six inches. I had doubted the word of my friend and came back to camp empty handed."

Dave Watson may have missed the catch there, but when it came to catching onto eternal life in Jesus Christ, his stringer is filled to overflowing. For a free booklet on the subject by Hank Parker called, "More Than Winning and Losing," contact us here at God's Great Outdoors" by mail, phone, or e-mail and we will also send you "The Ultimate Fishing Challenge," by Jim Grassi.

AN ENCAPSULATED MOMENT
FROM
"God's Great Outdoors"
#033

Early one bow season, the host of God's Great Outdoors, Gerry Caillouet had targeted Southeast Ohio's whitetail deer. The wooded hill's of Wayne National Forest produced a good crop of acorns that fed the resident deer population. Gerry had located a prime breeding area near a group of white oaks on the side of a flat ridge top. With a treestand placed between the oaks and the scrape, the action should prove exciting to say the least.

Having parked his car on the side of the road, Gerry readied himself by the dome light of the family station wagon. With sunrise less than an hour away, he needed to hurry. As he started off he chose to walk in the morning darkness, leaving his flashlight stored in his day pack. Soon his eyes adjusted and Gerry was able to see a few feet in front of him.

He found the well cleared trail at the base of the ridge he would be hunting and started to ascend. The trail was easy to follow until the vegetation became thicker, about a forth of the way up. Somehow in the steepness of the hill and the tangles of growth Gerry lost the trail. "I stopped and tried in my mind to retrace my progress. For one second I thought of pulling out my flashlight, but I was in a hurry and was sure I could find my way without the light," remembers Gerry.

Being sure he knew where the path was, he altered his course and pressed on. But, in no time Gerry was breaking through bush, with no trail to make the way easier. "Stopping again I chased away the idea for pulling out the flashlight. Now I was angry I hadn't used the light and had lost my way," add's Gerry. So, off he went busting his way up to a clear cut almost at the top. "The openness of the small clear cut allowed me to see just how far off to the right I had traveled. Then looking down I noticed a huge hole ripped in my brand new camouflage pants. Suddenly I saw that this was how I and many other Christians travel down the path of life." **God's Word Says In:** *Psalm 119:105 "Your Word is a lamp to my feet and a light for my path."*

Just as Gerry learned the value of a flashlight on the trail to his tree stand, we all need to learn the importance of opening the Bible each day, before and while we venture, into God's Great Outdoors.

ABOUT THE AUTHOR:

Gerry was born the 21st of April 1955 in New Orleans, Louisiana. The family were members of a denomination which taught that works helped receive God's grace and favor. The two most memorable years in Gerry's childhood were spent living on his grandparent's farm in Upstate New York. The woods, fields and streams were teaming with just about everything to capture a young boy's attention and interest. From there, the family moved to Laurel, Maryland and despite the relocation to the suburbs (15 miles from Washington, D.C.) Gerry hiked to the woods and fields surrounding his community. His expeditions were geared towards capturing creatures like crayfish, turtles, and salamanders.

Gerry's father instructed him in firearm safety, archery, and fly fishing. The family traveled to hunt and fish Maryland's Eastern Shore, mountains, and their home's neighboring hill country. Additionally, Gerry would spend summers visiting his older sister in the Upper Peninsula of Michigan. Here, he fished for pike and walleye all the while gazing across the water to the Canadian shoreline. All this stirred a desire for adventure in the outdoors.

With schooling complete, he joined the Marine Corps for some military adventure. Becoming more and more the rebel to the things of God and religious teachings, he would still drop in on church, but had no interest in it.

With his tour of duty over, Gerry continued on with his outdoor activities and the pursuit of another interest, girls. He and his wife Cyndi were married in 1976 and soon had their first son, Courtney. But their young marriage was floundering, and in truth the couple only stayed together because neither one could stand the thought of not being around their son.

A co-worker of Gerry's shared about his responsibility to care for a child's spiritual needs as well as the physical requirements. The young father was sure he would spend eternity in Hell and didn't care, but could not stand the thought of the same fate for his son, Courtney. So, Gerry began to seek the truth and accepted Jesus Christ as his Lord and Savior in March of 1978. Within two weeks his wife Cyndi received the Lord also. Soon their daughter, Katie was born followed less than two years later by son, Clinton. Over the years as Gerry has grown in Christ, there have been many tough lessons to learn and changes to be made. But God's Word supplies the transforming power to accomplish what we need to be changed to the likeness of God.

God turned Gerry's love of outdoor adventures into a desire to use those interests to reach the unsaved men, women, and children all around us who pursue the same activities. From a camping ministry at his home church, *Community Grace Brethren Church* in West Milton, Ohio, to working with *Christian Bowhunters of America* on both local and national level. This moved to an amazing series of doors the Lord opened to where Gerry now hosts and produces a nationally syndicated radio program called God's Great Outdoors.

How It All Started

If you ask me how the radio program of *God's Great Outdoors* came into being, be prepared to spend some time listening. Because as the story unfolds you'll discover God never takes us on a straight line from point A to point B. The Father must first prepare and change us. Thus, we travel on life's path through God's divine direction and always in His perfect timing.

In 1993, a group of men and women joined together and started a chapter of *Christian Bowhunters of America*. As the chapter grew and developed outreach programs, an idea for a hunt began to take shape. The hunt, called *The Trophies of Grace Whitetail Deer Hunt*, became the ministry's vision to see unsaved loved ones become the *"Trophies,"* not the deer that were harvested.

The hunt became an annual event with the second year seeing hunters and their families attend from nine different states. (The fifth annual hunt, saw twenty states represented.) Several weeks after the second hunt, I reflected on all the Christians who made their living in the outdoors. I also thought of all the different outdoor ministries I'd come in contact with the last few years. The Christian community needed to know about the sacrifices of both time and money that were being committed to reach unsaved outdoorsmen. Men, women, and children who will not attend church, listen to Christian radio, or watch Billy Graham on television, are finding Jesus Christ because of these Christians' efforts. With all this in mind the idea for a Christian radio program about God's great outdoors became a burning desire.

I approached my friend, who in 1994 still worked for *The CDR Radio Network*. On hearing my idea, Jon Skillman encouraged me to put it in writing to present to the station manager, Paul Gathnay. Paul gave the program idea a thumbs up and suggested I aim for a national airing, not just local. Jon also introduced me to Jim Leightenheimer, who teaches radio broadcasting at *Cedarville College*. Jim liked the program concept and was the major factor in getting the program off the ground. His time, expertise, and added ideas are the reason someone such as I, who knew nothing about radio production, is producing a nationally syndicated radio program today! Praise God!

With Jim's gifted help and answered prayers, the green light was given from Paul Gathnay. The fledgling program's first flight was July 6,1996, airing on *The CDR Radio Network*. At that airing, two underwriting sponsors began their commitment to the program's ministry: *API Outdoors, Inc.*, and *Black Widow Custom Bows, Inc.* Without these first two sponsors we would not be airing God's Great Outdoors today. Praise God!

The *National Religious Broadcasters Convention* in February of 1997 gave God's Great Outdoors, and the outdoor ministries we actively work with, the opportunity to network together. We united to have a booth in Washington, D.C.. This event allowed us to see what could happen if we worked as partners toward a common goal of reaching the unsaved sportsman. By also including the local church and the Christian media, we will only multiply the effectiveness. That is what the adventure part of the ministry is all about, life-style evangelism in God's great outdoors!

The program was also featured in the *National Religious Broadcasters* magazine which was quite an honor, considering I am someone who had no training in the field of radio broadcasting. It was quite humbling that the Lord allowed the program to be highlighted in such a prestigious Christian magazine.

Shortly after the *NRB Convention*, I lost my job of over fifteen years as the company downsized and relocated. My wife, Cyndi, and I felt God was moving us towards full-time ministry and seven months later she also lost her job and we were plunged into a walk of faith. In that period of time Cyndi took over the recipe portion of the program and with the loss of her job she took on the responsibility for the mounting office work that has been increasing with each month. This has all come about in our lives by the working of the Holy Spirit. Remember, I knew nothing about radio and am now hosting and producing a nationally syndicated Christian radio program! So, what can I say about how God's Great Outdoors came into being? Only this, **to God be the glory!**

"Expect great things from God, attempt great things for God."
William Carey

Where are they ....

I would like to say again that I am extremely grateful to these men who were willing to make themselves transparent. In relating mistakes that they have made we are all revealed as being equally human.

Of these men, some I have shared hunting camps with, or a day fishing. Others I have spent time getting to know at various outdoor shows or at their place of business. A few of the men I was introduced to where I had just brief meetings, long enough to do an interview with them. And a couple of these gentlemen I have only spoken to on the telephone. All of these men claim a personal relationship with their Lord and Savior Jesus Christ. I can tell you from time spent with some of these fellas, and creditable reports from mutual acquaintances on others, that their talk is reflected by their walk. But, I don't know their hearts, only Jesus who is going to judge us all knows their true position in Christ. However, the same thing is true for you and me. These men may falter on their journey with the Lord, yet if they have a personal relationship with Jesus Christ their position is secure. I hope after reading this book you can say the same thing.

If you would like to talk with any of these sportsmen for some kind of a speaking engagement or outreach we would be glad to help. Just contact us here at God's Great Outdoors and we will see what we can do.

ALL INFORMATION ON
God's Great Outdoors
8193 Emerick Road
West Milton, OH 45383

(937) 698-3656   Toll Free # 1-877-TALKGGO
E-Mail: ggoutdoors@aol.com   Web Site: www.ggoutdoors.org

To find out which stations air God's Great Outdoors visit our Web Site or listen any time on *ICRN.com*. Here you can hear the current weekly program and the last ten programs too! God's Great Outdoors radio program would not be possible without underwriters. To find out more about our underwriters or receive a catalog, visit out Web Site or write to:

Underwriters

Weatherby	*API Outdoors, Inc.*	*Mathews, Inc.*
3100 El Camino Real	P.O. Box 385	P.O. Box 709
Atascadero, CA 93422	Tallulah, LA 71282	Sparta, WI 54656
1-800-227-2009	1-800-228-4846	(608) 269-2728
Black Widow Bows, Inc.	*Hodgdon Powder Inc.*	*Sierra Trading Post*
1201 Eagle Crest	6231 Robinson	5025 Campstool Road
P.O. Box 2100	P.O. Box 2932	Cheyenne, WY 82007-1898
Nixa, MO 65714	Shawnee Missions, KS 66201	1-800-713-4534
(417) 725-3113	1-800-622-4366	

Why not join us on the **Trail To Adventure**
and become part of The Adventure Team!

The mission of God's Great Outdoors is to encourage the sharing of our interests in the outdoor adventures we enjoy with others. Thus, enabling our relationships to increase and provide a common ground from which to present the gospel of our Lord and Savior, Jesus Christ.

God's Great Outdoors radio program is a 501 (c) (3) ministry and is supported by outdoorsmen like you. Without financial support we cannot maintain daily operations or continue to add God's Great Outdoors to Christian radio stations across the nation.

Send your tax deductible donations to:
God's Great Outdoors,
8193 Emerick Road, West Milton, OH 45383

I want to become part of The Adventure Team!
"God's Great Outdoors"

NAME: _____

ADDRESS: _____

PHONE: _____ E-MAIL: _____

and

Please let us know how you enjoyed the book too!
We'll send you a free bookmark
Should man hunt, what does the bible say?

ALL INFORMATION ON
"God's Great Outdoors"

God's Great Outdoors
8193 Emerick Road
West Milton, OH 45383

(937) 698-3656
E-Mail: ggoutdoors@aol.com

Toll Free # 1-877-TALKGGO
Web Site: www.ggoutdoors.org

To find out which stations air God's Great Outdoors visit our Web Site or listen any time on *ICRN.com*. Here you can hear the current weekly program and the last ten programs too! God's Great Outdoors radio program would not be possible without underwriters. To find out more about our underwriters or receive a catalog, visit out Web Site or write to:

Underwriters

Weatherby
3100 El Camino Real
Atascadero, CA 93422
(805) 466-1767

API Outdoors, Inc.
P.O. Box 385
Tallulah, LA 71282
(318) 574-4903

Mathews, Inc.
P.O. Box 709
Sparta, WI 54656
(608) 269-2728

Black Widow Bows, Inc.
1201 Eagle Crest
P.O. Box 2100
Nixa, MO 65714
(417) 725-3113

Hodgdon Powder Inc.
6231 Robinson
P.O. Box 2932
Shawnee Missions, KS 66201
1-800-622-4366

Why not join us on the **Trail To Adventure**
and become part of The Advanced Team!

The mission of God's Great Outdoors is to encourage the sharing of our interests in the outdoor adventures we enjoy with others. Thus, enabling our relationships to increase and provide a common ground from which to present the gospel of our Lord and Savior, Jesus Christ.

God's Great Outdoors radio program is a 501 (c) (3) ministry and is supported by outdoorsmen like you. Without financial support we cannot maintain daily operations or continue to add God's Great Outdoors to Christian radio stations across the nation and beyond.

Send your tax deductible donations to:
God's Great Outdoors,
8193 Emerick Road, West Milton, OH 45383

I want to become part of The Advanced Team!
"God's Great Outdoors"

NAME: _____

ADDRESS: _____

PHONE: _____ E-MAIL: _____

and

Please let us know how you enjoyed the book too!